ENCORE

Strategies for Theatre Renewal

Judith Strong

*with a Foreword by Sir John Drummond
and chapter on Theatre Management
and Economics by Paul Iles*

Published by
The Theatres Trust Charitable Fund

Published by
The Theatres Trust Charitable Fund
22 Charing Cross Road
London WC2H 0HR

ISBN 0 9534675 0 3

Designed by Ray Carpenter
Typeset by Tom Knott
Printed by The Pale Green Press

FRONT COVER: Edinburgh Festival Theatre. (*Alan McCrone*)
FRONTISPIECE: The Stephen Joseph Theatre, Scarborough. (*Martine Hamilton Knight*)

Contents

The Mayflower Theatre, Southampton by architects W & T R Milburn
(1928) was originally known as *The Empire*.

During the middle years of this century Victorian and Edwardian theatres were often seen as relics of a past age. The decline in live entertainment and the growth of cinema and television also took their toll, and it was only when the great majority of these theatres had been lost that people began to realise how good some of them had been. Since then many of those that remained have been successfully restored, modernised and brought back to use.

This book tells some of their stories. It celebrates what has been achieved and demonstrates how it was done. We hope that it will provide encouragement to others.

The Theatres Trust is not simply concerned with conservation, for we recognise that there are many instances when it is better to put up a new building, and we are keen to encourage good standards of architecture and design. And if a good old theatre can no longer be used for its original purpose, we will try to ensure that an appropriate new use is found, and that any alterations do not preclude its potential one day to resume a theatrical life.

So the thirteen case studies in this book are not just about refurbishment for its own sake, but about how good theatre buildings have been kept going, or returned to theatrical life. The examples have been chosen to illustrate different types and scale of operation, and they also include two instances of theatres being created from other existing buildings – a chapel and a cinema. They illustrate the sort of alterations that may be necessary so that theatres can be modernised to meet the needs of the next century. They look at the strategies adopted, the skills that are needed, and the money that is needed – not just to renovate and maintain theatres – but also to fill them with good quality productions that will keep the audiences coming in and maintain them as places of live entertainment, stimulation and enjoyment.

It is significant that nearly all of the stories told here pre-date the National Lottery, and that where the influence of the lottery has been felt, it has not always been beneficial. Very few of our most important historic theatres have yet received funding from that source to enable full refurbishment schemes to go ahead. Fortunately, theatre buildings can attract considerable local interest and support, and the process of returning them to life can often be phased gradually over a long period and accomplished on a relative shoestring. It is not always necessary to do everything at once.

But it ought to be possible to do things better. The National Lottery was set up, and still has the potential to enable a properly planned national programme of refurbishment and renewal to be put in place. Such a task would probably take at least ten years to achieve. Nor should we forget that, once completed, a theatre will more than likely need revenue subsidy to help support a varied and worthwhile programme. What is needed is a reliable and continuing source of both capital and revenue funding for the arts, which enables people to plan ahead, and a system which offers them support and guidance while they are doing so. That is a task for Government and its arts agencies. On the evidence of this book the demand is there, as well as the energy and enthusiasm to make such a programme a success.

On behalf of The Theatres Trust I would like to congratulate Judith Strong for having produced this admirably clear and useful book. It is also eminently readable. Our thanks also go to Paul Iles, whose vast experience of theatre management is evident in his chapter. But the real heroes, as Judith generously points out in her introduction, are those whose efforts made possible the stories that are told in the pages which follow.

SIR JOHN DRUMMOND
Chairman of The Theatres Trust

From the programme for the
1895 Christmas production at the
Edinburgh Empire Palace Theatre.
Inset is H E Moss, founder of the
Moss Empire chain of theatres.

During the second half of the last century through into the first decade of this century, live entertainment – drama, variety, spectacle, music and opera – flourished in this country. Entrepreneurs saw it as a profitable investment and built theatres. In 1914, there were over one thousand. By the 1960s, about eighty-five per cent of these had been lost. Often valued only for the land on which they stood, many were demolished to make way for car parks, roads, shopping precincts and similar developments. Only about half of the theatre buildings which survived remained as places of live entertainment. Of the rest, some stood empty and neglected while others were used as cinemas, bingo houses, for pop music, as pubs, and even for storage – for anything from cars to second-hand furniture.

Eventually, people began to take notice. A review was carried out to establish the extent to which theatres were included on the Government's list of buildings of special architectural or historic interest. The *Save London Theatres Campaign* helped focus public attention and, in 1976, The Theatres Trust was established by Act of Parliament to promote the better protection of theatres for the benefit of the nation.

Over the last twenty years the loss of theatres has been stemmed and many have been restored, modernised and brought back to use. This book tells some of their stories. Its purpose is to celebrate what has been achieved; to demonstrate how it was done; and to provide encouragement to others.

Why save?

What is the point of saving these old theatres? Are the efforts to ensure their continued existence mere exercises in nostalgia or attempts to keep the buildings as 'museum' examples of a past age? Or can they have a genuine role as theatres? These studies show that they most definitely can.

Many of the Victorian and Edwardian theatres occupy good positions in town and city centres. Similar sites would not often be available for a new theatre. Some are buildings with strong individual character which have become part of the streetscape, well known and well liked by the local people. Each comes with its own history, eliciting memories of past performances and stimulating expectations of pleasures yet to be enjoyed. Research demonstrates that historic theatres attract more widely-based support and tend to have stronger 'Friends' organisations and more willing helpers than their contemporary equivalents (undertaken by Paul Iles when manager of *Blackpool Grand Theatre*). The case studies of the *Grand Theatre, Blackpool*, the *Georgian Theatre* in Richmond, Yorkshire and the *Hackney Empire* describe theatres which are very much a part of their local surroundings.

A well-designed and managed refurbishment scheme can also provide excellent value for money. The *Edinburgh Festival Theatre,* the *Stephen Joseph Theatre* in Scarborough and the *Mayflower* in Southampton all cost far less than the equivalent newly built spaces would have done.

Most importantly, these theatres have auditoria to be valued, not only for the richness of the interior decoration, but in the relationships they establish between performers and audience and between individuals within that audience. The Victorian and Edwardian 'boom' years gave the architects of the time the opportunity to develop and refine their ideas, and by and large they ended up by getting it right. (The most prolific of the Victorian theatre architects, Frank Matcham, designed over 150 theatres and had a hand in many more.) The theatres featured in these studies are all good spaces in which to perform, some are sensationally so.

Finding a role

One of the first points which this book sets out to demonstrate is the importance of identifying a role for the theatre which will enable it to establish itself in the local community, draw in audiences and attract the support it needs to be successful.

Finding the right role may not be easy. The theatres of this period (pre-1914), were in the main built as lyric houses for touring variety, opera and dance. They tend to be relatively large (1000–2000 seats) and to lack the workshop and storage spaces which a producing company would need. The problem is that many areas can only support one main touring theatre. The case studies on the *Tyne Theatre*, Newcastle and the *Edinburgh Festival Theatre* (with reference to the *King's Theatre*) illustrate this point. On the other hand, the study of the two Manchester theatres shows that one venue can be used to generate support for another.

Different groups have approached the problem in different ways. For example, the *Lancaster Grand* provides a home for its resident amateur company and a performing space for a whole range of other amateur groups within the area; *Blackpool Grand* operates a mixed programme of summer variety and 'off-season' tours of drama, dance, opera and musicals; the *Sheffield Lyceum* joined forces with the adjacent *Crucible* to provide a different style of theatre within a single organisation; while the *Theatre Royal, Glasgow* became the home of Scottish Opera. *Hackney Empire*, one of the best variety spaces in the country, pioneered the concept of 'New Variety', a contemporary mix of live entertainment well suited to its style and location.

Adapting the building

The early theatres were built to serve a very different age. Victorian society was essentially hierarchical, with its higher, middle and lower classes. This is reflected in the design of the theatres. The different seating areas were serviced by separate entrance routes and separate bars. Far more people were squeezed into the theatres than they are now licensed to accommodate. Those who sat up in the 'gods' were expected to queue in the street until they were allowed up the 'backstairs' route to the gallery. The economic success of these theatres depended on the income they could generate from ticket sales. The aim was to get a lot of people in (and out again once the show was over in time for a second house) as quickly as possible.

All this has changed. Audiences expect to have decent facilities whatever the price of the seat. Current theatre economics rely as much on the income from 'add-ons' as they do from ticket sales. In order to survive, theatres need the support of their local communities and so they seek to provide facilities which people can use throughout the day (bars and cafés, entertainment facilities, education spaces, etc). Each of the theatres featured in these studies has been reorganised or extended in some way to meet these new requirements. For the *Edinburgh Festival Theatre*, *Sheffield Lyceum* and *Bradford Alhambra* new front-of-house facilities have been built. In others, such as *Manchester Palace* and *Glasgow Theatre Royal*, additional space has been created by reorganising the existing interiors.

Production requirements have also changed. Many of the theatres featured in these studies rely on buying-in productions from visiting companies. Once again, economics dictate form. As Paul Iles explains in the section which follows, the touring companies tend to provide productions for particular sizes and styles of theatre. Those wanting a certain type of theatre 'product' (e.g. the large-scale musical) have to be able to provide the appropriate accommodation – in terms of stage size, technical equipment and 'get-in' (space for pantechnicons to deliver the sets, etc). Older theatres can be deficient in these areas, especially as more new theatres get built and others are refurbished to meet the higher standards.

Performers, too, need good conditions if they are to maintain a high quality of presentation. Dressing-rooms were often cramped in the old theatres, toilets minimal, showers non-existent. Few theatres provided any rehearsal facilities.

Legislation has also placed new responsibilities on theatre managers. Several of the studies make references to earlier theatres destroyed by fire. (In Edinburgh, the illusionist, Lafayette, inadvertently set fire to the curtains and died in the ensuing flames.) Health and Safety requirements are becoming increasingly demanding, requiring improvements to be made even in the recently refurbished theatres. Legislation (and lottery grant criteria) also covers accessibility for disabled people. Many of the old theatres have narrow stepped entrances and circuitous routes from foyer to auditorium which make it difficult for people to get around. The studies show how different theatres have tackled these problems.

The skills to do the job

Several of the case studies tell stories of groups of volunteers clearing debris, stripping equipment left by previous users, and clambering up ladders to repaint the interiors. Some of the theatres were initially brought back into use by salvaging seating, lighting and equipment from other venues. But sooner or later, they all discover that the 'brush and bucket' approach only takes them so far. Eventually, the basic problems have to be tackled. For this they need two things: money and the expertise to ensure that it is well spent.

Theatres are complex buildings. Like a factory, they have to house a 'production process'; provide facilities for the workers, and present the finished product. In addition to this, they have to service an audience and create the ambience and special relationships between that audience and the performance which some describe as the 'magic' of the theatre. Designing these spaces requires both creative skill and specialist expertise. Changing spaces which others have designed is only effective if it is done by people who understand why the original architects took the decisions they did.

The listing procedure which has helped to save many historic theatres (see page 00) can affect the way in which these theatres are being refurbished, though past case histories have established a reasonably lenient attitude to rebuilding stage houses and extending the front of house as several of these studies show. The facilities described in the previous section all have to be fitted into what are often historic structures and their adjacent sites, without destroying the authenticity of the original. The case study of the *Georgian Theatre*, Richmond looks at the issues involved. Though this could be seen as an extreme case (a unique survival, listed grade I) many other listed theatres have to find ways of solving similar problems. In the *Edinburgh Festival Theatre*, for example, new ventilation systems were fitted behind the decorative panelling, and when the *Glasgow Theatre Royal* was being redecorated, old catalogues were scoured to identify replacement fittings for the foyers and the auditorium.

This book illustrates the range of expertise that is available both within the design and conservation fields. The Theatres Trust publishes a series of advisory notes (see bibliography, page 103) and is able to help put people in touch with the relevant advisory and consultancy bodies.

The case studies

The fourteen theatres featured (in thirteen separate studies) have been selected to provide examples of different types of operation in different parts of the country. Most arts buildings (including theatres) are either owned by a trust or owned by a local authority and leased to a trust which has responsibility for the whole operation. However, examples are included in these studies of commercially owned and managed venues and of a theatre run directly by the local authority. Some produce their own work, more depend on touring product. A few rely on amateur productions. Some mix several styles of operation. The

---

MR. KEAN'S
Second Night of Engagement

THEATRE ROYAL, RICHMOND.

On Tuesday Evening, September 6th. 1819.

Will be Presented Colman's celebrated Play of the

IRON CHEST,

The Part of Sir Edward Mortimer by Mr. KEAN,

Fitzharding	Mr. SAUNDERS,	Robber	Mr. STOKER,
Willford	Mr. BUTLER,	Boy	Miss L. STOKER,
Adam Winterton	Mr. GEORGE,		
Samson	Mr. HODGSON,	Helen	Miss BUTLER,
Orsor	Mr. JEFFERSON,	Blanch	Mrs. HODGSON,
Armstrong	Mr. BROWN,	Barbara	Mrs. SAUNDERS,

A Comic Song by Mr. HODGSON
A Dance by Mrs. Saunders.

To conclude with a favourite Farce, called

How to Die for Love,

Baron	Mr. BROWN,	Trap	Mr. HODGSON,
Captain Bloomenfield	Mr. BUTLER,	Bricklayer	Mr. GEORGE,
Captain Thalwick	Mr. SAUNDERS,		
Trick	Mr. JEFFERSON,	Charlotte	Miss BUTLER.

In consideration of the difficulty of obtaining the above unrivalled Performer, at this period, the great request he is in, and the high terms which the display of his talent commands, it is hoped the following advance of the prices of admission will not be objectionable.

BOXES 4s —— PIT 3s —— GALLERY 1s. 6d.

N. B. The three top seats of the Pit the price of the Boxes

Doors to be opened at six and to begin at seven o'Clock.

(The Georgian Theatre Trust)

original buildings date from 1782 to 1928. All are currently used as theatres, though two were originally built for other purposes: one a cinema (*Stephen Joseph Theatre*, Scarborough), the other a Salvation Army citadel (*Chipping Norton Theatre*).

When theatres hit the headlines it is usually because of some particular success or some 'scandalous' failure. The events between tend to go unrecorded. These studies set out to tell the longer story, outlining the strategies which led to that success and the situations which may have resulted in problems but, in many cases, have gone on to be satisfactorily resolved. Above all, they aim to demonstrate that keeping a theatre live is a continuing process involving constant adaptation to changing circumstances.

The studies concentrate on three particular aspects: the campaigns which gave these theatres a new lease of life; the work which was done to refurbish and improve the buildings; and the management and programming strategies which have succeeded in securing their future.

A quick glance at the section headings in the studies will show that there are common threads running through all stories – early success, decline, possibly bingo or some other use, rescue and revival. But there is no standard pattern, no model which can be followed to ensure success. Every theatre is different. Each one has had to find out how best to operate within its own particular circumstances.

Though the studies could be regarded as success stories, they do not simply record the successes. All the theatres featured in these studies have had to struggle to re-establish themselves and several of them have failed at some point and had to start all over again. By the time this book is published, at least one of the theatres could even have closed (but will, it is hoped, be opened again).

One of the objectives of The Theatres Trust in publishing this book is to encourage those who have a direct or indirect responsibility for a theatre to consider the longer term, and to offer support through difficult periods in order to secure the building and the activities it houses, for the future.

Protective legislation

Though a great number of theatre buildings have been lost, many remain. Early cinemas were also designed to take live shows, just in case 'moving pictures' failed to find an audience after the initial novelty had worn off. Many of these are now closed, struggling to survive against the new multi-screens, or housing a declining bingo operation. Some will have good auditoria and occupy town/city centre sites.

These studies demonstrate that opportunities have to be grasped. Few, if any, of the buildings featured in these studies stood empty for long – on the market and waiting for a buyer. Three separate attempts to buy the *Sheffield Lyceum* failed when others got in first with a bid. Either for the land they occupy or for the interior space they offer, theatre buildings tend to attract interest.

How can they be protected so that the potential remains for them to be reopened?

While theatres, as such, have no special protection against demolition, inappropriate use or neglect, planning legislation can be used to 'buy time', put pressure on owners and influence what they do to their buildings. In certain instances it can require

them to undertake structural repairs. Detailed information on the relevant legislation and how it can be used is set out in The Theatres Trust Advice Note No. 3 'Theatre preservation'. What follows here is only a summary.

One important special provision affecting theatres is contained in the General Development Order 1995 (and its Scottish equivalent) which requires all local planning authorities to consult The Theatres Trust before granting planning permission affecting 'any land on which there is a theatre'. This means any theatre, new or old, used or disused. The operative word, however, is 'consult' (which is not the same as 'notify'). Although the Trust does not have the power to direct an authority to refuse planning permission or to impose conditions, its expert advice does carry weight. There are several studies in this book which demonstrate the role played by the Trust. The requirement to consult proved crucial in the case of the *Sheffield Lyceum*.

Most important of all the potentially protective legislation is that given to listed buildings. If a theatre is listed, then listed building consent will be needed for demolition or alterations which affect its 'special architectural or historic interest'. Applications for listed building consent are considered against criteria produced by Central Government (PPG 15 Planning and the Historic Environment deals with the situation in England) as well as conservation policies drawn up by the local authorities in the area in which the building is sited. Applications for demolition, or for any works to buildings listed grade I or II★ (in England and Wales) have to be referred to the local office of the appropriate Government department, which will then seek advice from the national heritage bodies.

The principle behind the legislation is one of 'managing change' rather than prohibiting alteration. The essence of the approach is to identify what is important about the existing building and to strike a balance between preserving the original fabric, recognising its overall significance and historic integrity, and works which are necessary for the building to continue in use. It is generally held that the best use for a building is the one for which it was originally designed.

All the buildings in these case studies are listed (except for one – the small theatre at Chipping Norton). Examples of how the legislation was used and the protection it gave, are set out in the studies of the *Grand Theatre*, Blackpool, the *Mayflower* in Southampton and the Lancaster *Grand Theatre*. The study of the *Stephen Joseph Theatre* in Scarborough demonstrates that listed building consent may be given to allow significant changes to be made when these are considered to be necessary to secure a future for the building.

The third area of planning legislation which has served

to protect theatres is that relating to 'change of use'. The use of land and buildings and the design of new buildings (and most extensions and additions to existing buildings), is controlled by the relevant local authority under the terms of the Town and Country Planning legislation. Responsibilities are shared between Borough, District, Unitary and County Councils. These authorities have drawn up structure plans and local plans which set out how different areas will be used. Many areas will be designated for a certain type of use, such as housing, light industry or commercial. Individual buildings also fall within a particular specified category of use defined in a *Use Classes Order* (UCO). If the owner wishes to change the use of a building to a use which falls outside the category in which it is placed, planning permission must be secured.

An application for a change of use can pose a threat in a number of ways. Theatre buildings which are being used as theatres are protected by being part of no class (i.e. there are no other uses to which a theatre can be put without planning permission being sought). Once change of use has been granted, it permits further changes to be made within the designated UCO without further need for planning permission. A change-of-use application could be submitted to allow a use which might seem reasonably compatible with that of live entertainment but which, if granted, could open the door to a range of far less acceptable uses.

Some planning applications are made for change of use only, with no reference to works. This is where the major threat to theatre buildings lies. Physical changes almost invariably follow changes of use. There are several examples within these case studies of the legislation being used to limit alterations being made to the interior of an old theatre, to those which could be easily reversed should an opportunity arise in the future to reinstate the theatre use. The first three studies illustrate the planning negotiations in most detail.

Pressure groups and trusts

While individuals are often best able to initiate action, long-term success depends on building up a firm base and establishing a network of support, both from organisations which can influence decisions and people with time or skills to offer. Even at the start of a campaign, the pressure of numbers can help sway a decision. In several of these studies, one of the first steps towards saving a theatre was a petition. The studies of *Blackpool Grand* and the *Hackney Empire* demonstrate how effective group action can be.

As soon as a group begins to consider appointing staff or consultants or to explore the possibility of acquiring a building, it needs to be constituted on a legal basis. Arts organisations, as these studies show, are usually managed by either a trust or by a non-profit distributing company. A trust has the disadvantage of leaving the trustees with a personal responsibility for ensuring that the operation is viable so most theatres now opt for the company format.

Whichever way the managing body is constituted, the question of charitable status needs to be considered as this confers a number of benefits. These include tax concessions (charities can reclaim tax related to covenants and gifts), rate relief and eligibility for grant aid. While theatre ownership and production would be regarded as charitable activities by the Charitiy Commission, many theatres have other interests (such as catering) which have to be conducted by a commercial trading company (but that trading company need not pay tax on its profits if it convenants them to the charity or pays them through gift aid).

Both property ownership and theatre production involve elements of risk, as several of these studies show. Many organisations now separate the theatre ownership from the theatre activities so that each is safeguarded from losses incurred by the other. (The Manchester theatres and the *Tyne Theatre* studies both record property deals which have resulted in the whole operation ending up in the hands of the receiver.)

Balancing the books

It was tempting to close some of the studies at the point where the paint had just dried and the corks from the gala opening were still scattered around. But a refurbished building, however beautiful and well equipped, is only a serviced shell. To be a theatre, a place of live entertainment, it needs plays, musicals, ballet, opera, comedy and shows good enough to draw in audiences, not just for the opening event but night after night and year after year. Mounting such a programme requires skill – the ability to gauge and engage the audience, balancing the need to excite and stimulate with an assurance that their money will be well spent and that they will enjoy 'a good night out'. But even capacity audiences do not of themselves ensure financial viability. Ticket prices very rarely cover the costs involved in running a theatre, as these studies demonstrate. Some of the theatres do manage a break-even operation for much of the time (and the occasional profit), but even the successful ones may need to be underwritten when they hit a bad year. Most others, efficiently run but operating in different markets, depend on a regular subsidy as part of their income.

The case studies give information on the levels of subsidy

which the individual theatres need to support their operating costs. These should not be regarded as 'league tables'. The circumstances in which each theatre operates (the seating capacity, support facilities, catchment areas, and competition from other venues), vary greatly as do their programmes. What is a successful proportion of income to expenditure in one, could represent failure in another.

The economics of theatre production are examined in detail by Paul Iles (page 16).

Role of local authorities

During the middle decades of this century, local authorities bought or built theatres and proceeded to manage them. These theatres now tend to be the exception. *Bradford Alhambra* is the only example of a local authority managed space featured in this book though several of the others are owned by the local authority but leased to trusts. In such cases the authority has either secured (through application to EC or Government sources) or provided (from their own resources) the bulk of the money needed to buy and refurbish the buildings. One example is the *Mayflower* in Southampton. The case studies also show how some local authorities have set up consortia or encouraged separate theatres to work as a single entity (Bradford, Sheffield and Edinburgh).

Local authorities have tools, other than money, which can be used to retain a theatre building. One of these is the planning legislation. Another is the influence which they can bring to bear on funding organisations for both the arts and heritage interests. They are also able to provide both professional and advisory services.

Local authorities have another longer-term role: that of helping support the theatres when in operation. Most of the theatres featured in these studies (and theatres generally) need revenue support. Some authorities providing regular subsidy see themselves as patrons; others do so to secure live entertainment and related facilities for the community. There is also a case to be made for regarding money spent on supporting a theatre as an investment which can be justified by the additional income its activities generate and by the employment opportunities it provides (both within its organisation and in the surrounding area). When local authorities look at the theatres in the wider context, they find good reasons for putting money into them. The studies of the *Bradford Alhambra* and the *Mayflower* in Southampton both illustrate this approach. The study of *Edinburgh Festival Theatre* makes reference to a detailed economic regeneration cost benefit analysis which was carried out both

before the theatre was reopened and after the first year of its operation.

Paying for the building costs

As these studies show, saving a theatre can be a very long process. Very occasionally the possibility exists to pull the whole thing together and make one big effort to buy a theatre and put it to rights. More often it is a case of working step by step to achieve a long-term objective. Several of the studies outline projects which took thirty years or more to bring to fruition.

Even when the money for a major refurbishment has been found, the building still needs to be maintained. Looking after an historic theatre is a continuing process. Redecorating an ornately detailed and gilded auditorium or a stuccoed exterior is expensive. Maintaining these theatres costs money – more money than most of them are able to raise through their day-to-day activities.

Sources of funding, on the other hand, tend to come and go. The Arts Council's Housing the Arts Fund ran for sixteen years 1969 to 1985, though, towards the end of this period, the funds available were very limited. Since then, there have been two other initiatives directed towards arts buildings: the short-lived Theatres Restoration Fund, set up by the Government in April 1991 in association with the Wolfson Foundation and Family Charitable Trust, and the National Lottery set up in 1994 with the Arts Councils of the four constituent part of the United Kingdom each being defined as a distributory body. The Theatres Restoration Fund lasted two years, while the National Lottery ran for three years before reductions in its initially very generous allocation of money forced it to cut back, leaving those who were less than quick off the mark to revise their strategies. The recipients of the larger-scale lottery grants featured in these studies were those who already had projects either planned and waiting for further funding or already partially completed. Several others, starting from scratch, only got as far as the feasibility stage before the cuts struck, while some are still at the initial (and all important) 'thinking' stage.

Theatres use whatever capital resources they can lay their hands on – employment programmes, urban regeneration initiatives, planning gain, schemes to boost tourism, projects to provide better access for the disabled, money to maintain historic structure – they have all made a contribution over the years. These sources are still used to provide the 'partnership' element of lottery-funded projects. It is not coincidental that a high proportion of theatres featured in these studies are in development areas. They serve to demonstrate how reliant the

SAVE THE HACKNEY EMPIRE. AFTER ALL IT SAVED THIS LOT.

FOR MORE INFORMATION CALL THE HACKNEY EMPIRE APPEAL ON 0181 985 8844.

arts have been on EC and UK Government job creation and urban regeneration schemes.

As Sir John Drummond argues in the preface to this book, what is needed is a reliable and continuing source of both capital and revenue funding for the arts, which enables people to plan ahead and offers them support and guidance while they are so doing.

Importance of individuals

The research for these studies involved going through files of documents: records, reports, correspondence, press cuttings and theatre histories. Again and again, the crucial role which individuals had played leapt out of the pages. Peter Longman, the Arts Council's first Housing the Arts Officer and now Director of The Theatres Trust writes in one such letter 'Ultimately in this business, although one talks about buildings and organisations, it is the people behind them that one is assessing and in whom one invests. People can make seemingly impossible things happen.'

Within these studies, there are several examples of individual actions which have resulted in the 'saving' of the buildings. There are also references to people who have worked year after year first to secure and then maintain the buildings. Some have rushed in just at the moment when action was needed; others have carefully and patiently planned the best route forward. This book can be read as a record of their achievement, of the enthusiasm, skills, and dedication of the huge cast of theatre impresarios, financiers, performers, conservationists, historians, architects, engineers, builders, fundraisers, grant-givers, philanthropists, volunteers and supporters who, over two centuries, have created and sustained these buildings as centres of live entertainment. Without them none of these theatres would exist.

'Vision' is rather an overworked term in the current arts climate, but taking a rundown building and re-creating a live theatre takes vision. Somebody needs to be able to conceive what could be achieved, believe that the whole process is worthwhile, and care sufficiently to make it happen.

Looking at these theatres today, with their refurbished auditoria and wide-ranging programmes, many people might think that their success was a foregone conclusion. They would be wrong. Virtually all the theatres featured in these studies were written off at some point in their lives. Those who spent time, effort and money bringing them back to life took some enormous risks. Fortunately, they were people who had the courage to face up to criticism when problems occurred and the determination to keep on going.

Acknowledgements

These case studies were compiled from information contained in documents which The Theatres Trust has on file; appeal brochures, history books, annual accounts, programmes and press releases begged or borrowed from the theatres featured in these studies; visits to the theatres; discussions with present and past managers and artistic directors; and advice from the Trust's officers and from other specialist consultants. (Where particular publications have been used, they are referenced either in the text or at the end of each study.)

I would like to express my thanks to all those who helped me piece the stories together and my admiration for the hundreds of others whose contributions they record.

Judith Strong September 1998

'The glorious uncertainty of the boards almost rivals that of the turf'

Jerome K Jerome, *On the Stage – and Off*, 1885

How are theatres restored and organised, how do they grow? If one could run through in quick review the history of all the ventures that have been launched this century, I doubt if two theatres could be found with an identical origin and development. Their fabrics themselves, as shown in these case studies, have seen countless vagaries of fortune. Their organisation is equally diverse.

Theatres usually operate either by housing a company which creates the productions – a producing theatre – or by providing a stage for a series of visiting companies: the touring theatre or 'receiving house'.[1] The majority of case studies in this book are examinations of touring theatres, each of them buying-in shows for different programme mixes and lengths of run. (Other operations include the Stephen Joseph Theatre in Scarborough, run by a producing company which, like many repertory theatres today, also presents some visiting artists and companies; the Lancaster Grand Theatre which is the home of an amateur company; and the Theatre Royal, Glasgow, owned and operated by Scottish Opera).

Two key areas need to be addressed by theatre management. Artistic decisions about the choice of production, actors' performances and the physical setting occupy the foreground. The background is concerned with the social and financial context in which a theatre operates as an institution. It is these non-artistic conventions that are the subject of this chapter. There is, however, a middle ground where the two areas meet. This is especially true in a theatre which presents touring productions, where the manager has to find a successful and continuous combination of drama, dance, ballet, opera, musicals, concerts and light entertainment. Audience taste will change, and a stable audience may become a highly vocal public, bored with the same experiences. Thus, even the most successful theatre must change its diet of companies from time to time. Prosperity is never assured. The critical element in theatre management is,

therefore, an understanding of the nature of the community of which the theatre is a part, coupled with the ability to create an environment conducive to enabling artists to reach their full expression.

There has been a change in structure and management – a gradual shift in control of theatres from those which are run by artists and theatre makers to those local authorities or non-profit trusts which are, hopefully, knowledgeable and motivated by a love of theatre. The art of the theatre and the politics of subsidy tend to be the current preoccupation of producing theatres, which are usually led by value-driven beliefs, whereas the box-office and the core business of theatre management are the principal factors in determining success in most touring theatres. To understand how these changes came about, we need to look at the history of theatre management.

An industrial revolution in the theatre: producing theatres and touring theatres

A characteristic of the organisation of producing theatres is decentralisation, with theatres run as independent entities for their communities. The forerunner of this repertory theatre model was the stock ensemble of the eighteenth and nineteenth centuries, over which actor-managers had complete control, often playing leading roles themselves, surrounding themselves with other resident actors and occasional visiting stars. Having their own company meant that there was little inducement to establish business relationships with other theatres and, in turn, these had nothing to offer to a stock company. They were entirely self-sufficient, with their own actors under their own management, both in production and administration. They owned their sets, properties and wardrobe. They did not even have to look for plays to produce, for besides the standard classical dramas that were in the repertoire, they could, in the absence of adequate copyright legislation, readily obtain, at low cost, pirated versions of newer successes.

Each case study is about a provincial theatre, except for the Hackney Empire Theatre. Historically, theatre in Britain has been perceived largely as a view of the London stage, despite the fact that there has always been a vast amount of activity in the regions. Revolutionary political, social and economic changes brought about the decline of stock companies in the 1880s. Theatre going assumed a class division with the growth of industrial cities, especially in the North. Music halls began and big profits could be made on smaller outlays in variety theatre. The railway network brought entire touring companies to perform in these big new theatres, making the stock companies redundant and London dominant. The breakdown of the stock company system and its replacement by touring changed the character of theatre economics, as completely as the advent of power machinery and the evolution of the factory system had changed the character of manufacturing industry. It is therefore possible to speak of an 'industrial revolution' in the theatre, since this term suggests all that is inferred in a shift from resident theatres to touring. Touring caused the separation of theatre buildings and theatre production. One is quite as important as the other. Neither can succeed without the other, but the building infrastructure became a different element in theatrical management and today the two strands of theatre usually require separate subsidies.

Many of the case study theatres were built at the end of the last century, when 'bricks and mortar' management became, from an economic point of view, the dominant factor in theatre business. At various times in the history of theatre management the balance of power shifts between the theatre building interests and those of the producer. The reasons for this are pertinent to the organisation of the industry today. The first reason why 'bricks and mortar' may be the dominant interest is that a theatre is relatively permanent while a production is of very short duration. Theatres, of course, do not last forever (and frequently burned down in the 1800s) but six months on the road is a long life for a touring production. In short, the stability of the theatre is, as against the instability of the production, the first factor in the favour of buildings. When the stock company system finished and, later in the twentieth century, the subsidised repertory theatres lost the relative security and continuity of a resident company, there followed a new focus on theatre buildings. The second reason is concentration of control: the extensive Moss' Empires and Howard and Wyndham circuits were attractive to new investors and threw the balance of control in their favour as the circuits expanded. This has recurred in the 1990s with the expansion of Apollo Leisure's chain of touring theatres. A No. 1 theatre[2] in a big city called for a large investment of capital, while a big production required a relatively small amount of investment. A theatre building was considered to be a more stable investment than production, and for that reason attracted capital more readily.

However, there were counteracting factors to steer capital towards productions. In the first place, a production held out the promise of a tremendous profit in relation to the investment. After the Copyright Act of 1911 and the rise of cinema, live theatre held out the possibility of picture rights, foreign rights, and overseas touring rights in addition to the profit of the original production. Big successes were rare, but there were always possibilities to lure the investor. Moreover, it has always been the production and not the theatre building which holds the glamour. The natural tendency for buildings to dominate the theatre business is often interrupted by market conditions. Theatre chains, whether Moss' Empires[3] yesterday or Apollo Leisure today, have to be careful to check an oversupply of theatres in relation to the supply of productions, for there may not then be enough good (meaning popular) attractions to fill the touring circuit. The construction of big new Arts Council National Lottery financed lyric theatres such as the Lowry Centre Salford, the Regent Theatre in Stoke-on-Trent, the Milton Keynes Theatre, Bristol Harbourside Centre, the enlarged Sadler's Wells Theatre and the Wales Millennium Centre in Cardiff is increasing the size of the national circuit: it is a serious challenge to administer, for more theatres have to be continually supplied with attractions.

A good relationship between theatres and production companies is vital, for although producers choose to make their living by sending productions on tour, they do not *need* to produce a show in the way that a theatre *must* present one: a producer's standing costs while doing nothing are generally lower than those of a dark theatre. This might give underlying financial advantage to producers in negotiating terms with theatres, but a theatre should be more knowledgeable about its audience and market than producers. A chain of theatres, such as Apollo Leisure[4] or Ambassador Theatre Group, can reduce the producers' advantage by offering more than one date, thereby giving their theatres a financial advantage which allows for stable conditions in contracting productions.

To counteract the vagaries of finding attractions, non-profit touring theatres are sometimes associated with 'resident' companies.[5] Nevertheless, theatres managed as individual organisations encounter increasing difficulties in competing for the best shows and, therefore, usually require local authority subsidy.[6] There are only a few exceptions, notably the Mayflower Theatre

Southampton (a well-managed monopoly theatre with a large catchment which made a surplus of £313,426 in 1997),[7] the Birmingham Hippodrome (at the centre of an enormous population, making a surplus of £846,966 in 1996),[8] the Theatre Royal Bath (at the centre of a wealthy catchment which is willing to pay London ticket prices) and Blackpool Grand Theatre (sustained by an annual eighteen weeks, twice-nightly summer variety season).

Business management

The theatre must be carried on as a business or it will fail as an art. A theatre is not the easiest thing to manage: it needs foresight, tact, urbanity, thrift, good taste, eternal vigilance and, above all, the support of the public.

– Sir Henry Irving, 1889

The deal with producers is foundational to financial success. It is a principal cause of the financial difficulties or failure of many touring theatres singly managed by local authorities or independent trusts. Separation of the function of theatre ownership from that of production has created an area of competition within the theatre: the division of receipts from the attraction, and in terms of the other terms of engagement. Furthermore, every touring theatre is potentially the competitor of every other theatre in respect of the production it wants at the time it wants it, so the negotiation of favourable terms is paramount: a theatre must retain as much of the box office income as possible.

Most touring theatre management practice is preoccupied with receipts. Cash is more important than the recording of seat numbers sold, whereas subsidised theatres report to local authority and arts funding agencies who are also interested in attendance statistics. Running a touring house is a high-risk, cash oriented business, even when standing costs are strictly controlled and minimised. The link between theatres and producers is effected by the contract, whereby a production occupies a stage for a period of time, with the parties dividing box-office income and certain expenditures with terms agreed upon.

The cycle of tour organisation begins by 'pencilling dates', which can develop into chaos if no specific time is allotted to a 'pencilling'. It is courtesy and custom that given a reasonable period no 'pencilling' is erased by the theatre manager until calling the producer to declare a confirmation or otherwise. When a producer is booking a tour and suddenly has an important date cancelled peremptorily, it may cause much trouble and expense, such as jumping from Aberdeen to Plymouth and back to Edinburgh; conversely, a manager might see a lot of good pro-

ductions pass by for a date only to be told that, after several months, when too late to book another good production, the 'pencilling' is off.

During the 'pencilling' period, the parties will begin negotiation for terms. Modelling, in a theatre's estimates, is built upon a range of contract possibilities beginning with 'box-office splits', with risk thereby shared between the theatre and producer. Until the 1960s, when most No. 1 theatres were commercially owned and most productions were unsubsidised, the division of box-office income was usually sixty per cent in favour of the producer, whereas seventy per cent going to the producer is today's theorem. The actual share varies significantly from production to production and from theatre to theatre. The producing company often asks the theatre manager for a 'guarantee', or fee, which it would receive irrespective of the level of box-office receipts and, usually, on account of its share. Often royalties are paid to the producing company 'off-the-top', on behalf of the creative team of author, director, set, costume and lighting designers and, additionally, the tour-booker: these can total twenty-two per cent for musicals. This form of contract is the highest risk to the theatre.[9]

The parties may be prepared to negotiate this into a 'first-call' on the box-office receipts rather than a guaranteed fee. In this case, when the producing company's costs are not achieved, they would be losing money, and the theatre would receive no income to redeem overheads. When agreeing to either a guarantee or a first call, the theatre should be in a position to agree a higher 'second call' on the box-office receipts than may be represented by thirty per cent or a sum in excess of the theatre's standing costs. For the theatre this is return for taking the risk of paying a guarantee or first call. Theatres achieve widely varying positive annual margins, ranging from zero to about twenty-three per cent in the best managed. They need to develop a trusting contractual relationship with many producing companies so that both parties are confident of predicting the potential performance for their attractions. Slippage of the annual margin invariably occurs when theatres consistently pay guarantees, because however experienced the parties are they cannot, in reality, anticipate success. Only one or two failures will plunge a theatre into debt from which it is very hard to recover from future margins and other trading income. A tough approach from the manager is critical to the operation, developing a portfolio of deals with the theatre's board or a finance committee monitoring them carefully.

Contractual negotiations also include detailed arrangements for shared marketing expenditure and agreed items to be re-charged to producing companies. These number at least forty potential categories in the 'contra account', such as get-in, fit-up, the supply of performance stage-staff, rehearsals, get-out and piano tuning. The main heads of a standard contract were agreed upon some years ago by the Theatrical Management Association: they publish a basic form for modern management, which may be cited for as a groundwork for adaptation, local conditions being different in every case. The theatres also operate barring clauses, for period and distance, limiting competition from tours to adjacent towns. These interdictions often seem unnecessary: in reason, can Edinburgh bar Glasgow or Kirkcaldy? Can Manchester bar Salford or Blackpool? Or naturally, vice versa.

The experience of contracts, and their link to realising the theatre's artistic programme, stands testimony to the pressures and contradictions of trying to wrestle the ground between commerce and art, and this tension will ebb and flow through the operation of all theatres. They are all fraught with a very high degree of risk – but that is by no means the same as saying that they are gambling enterprises. Those managers who are skilled succeed in reducing the percentage of risk against them. On the other hand, those managers who are unskilled increase the natural hazards and this may, in part, account for the large subsidies required in some touring theatres run by local government controlled trusts or leisure departments.[10] (Because of their size, local authorities have differences in organisational culture and their financial systems are often unhelpful to the smaller world of theatres which have to be more entrepreneurial.) Whatever the deal with producers, there will be an appreciable element of risk for everyone. It is innate in the touring system and there is no insurance against it. There is no theatre and no producing company which has stayed in business for any length of time which has not suffered some downright failures!

The programme mix

The art of popular theatre is a permanent revolution.

– Jean Vilar, *Theatre as Public Service*, 1953

The programming of touring theatres is guided by a number of important factors. These include the aspirations of a theatre's mission statement and a definable artistic policy, its known theatregoing market, the availability of productions, the size of the stage, the potential box-office receipts and the energy and aspirations of the manager. There never was, and there never will be, an ideally programmed theatre. Theatres are too complex and delicate a machine, depending on the harmonious co-operation of too many talents and influences, ever to reach perfection for more than a passing moment. Good theatres at their best periods have been severely criticised, not, as a rule, without reason. The

following table is a summary of the programme mix at the 937-seat Buxton Opera House, a good example of a local authority owned, non-profit trust managed theatre.[11] Over eighty distinct productions are staged annually. The theatre's policy cites the eight demands and tastes of audiences as defined by John McGrath, offering 'directness, comedy, music, emotion, variety, effect, immediacy and localism'.[12]

Buxton Opera House Programme Mix, 1997–8

Art form	No. of perfs. staged	Seats sold	% capacity	Theatre's margin retained	% of perfs. per art form
Ballet	8	3500	47%	24%	3.0%
Classical concerts	6	3680	65%	24%	2.4%
Modern dance	1	277	29%	20%	0.4%
Children & panto	31	16,661	57%	27%	12.2%
Other dance	10	2614	28%	16%	3.9%
Drama	81	17,184	23%	14%	31.8%
Folk and jazz	5	2602	56%	24%	2.0%
Light entertain.	41	21,729	55%	23%	16.1%
Music theatre	43	20,563	51%	28%	16.9%
Opera	29	20,368	75%	15%	11.4%
Hires	6				
Totals	261	109,178	45%	21%	100.0%

Theatres' ability to programme is affected, additionally, by the Arts Councils and, in England, the Regional Arts Boards, who take a strategic stance on the cities and towns to be played by funded companies: many of the productions in Buxton are subsidised by the Arts Council of England Touring Department. Touring theatres have been neglected by the arts funding system, with almost all revenue grants going to the producing company – but marketing, ticket pricing, press relations, audience development, outreach and education practice are a shared responsibility of a company and a theatre. Theatres welcome the introduction of small 'venue development grants' from the Touring Department, for whatever the terms of contract with a producer (unless the company is renting the theatre on a 'four walls' contract), the theatre is also speculating on the success of the attraction.

Organisation, staffing and overheads

One must never underrate the importance in the theatre of the machinery of organisation and staff. Think not of plans but of persons.

– Harley Granville Barker, *The Exemplary Theatre*, 1922

Now a few words on the costs of running a theatre. Theatre costs are of two kinds – overhead expenditure and running costs. The former are fixed charges which must be met whether the theatre is idle or has a production. Touring theatres generally expect to be open year round (perhaps closed for two weeks' annual maintenance or for part of the summer) and therefore merge these costs into 'overheads'. The chief item might be rent, but non-profit theatre operators outside London tend to be lessees whose local authority owners waive such charges, but may expect the non-profit distributing company to cover repairs.

The biggest cost is staffing, but there is an enormous variation in personnel, due partly to differences in size of theatre but also to differences in the requirements of the productions and whether or not the theatre is engaged in new arts objectives and occupations such as education, outreach, workshops or access schemes. The following is an organisation chart for Buxton Opera House. It has a full-time staff of sixteen, a part-time staff of twenty-two and a pool of volunteers for front-of-house stewarding. Most touring theatres are staffed with minor variants to this structure, which sets out a clear management framework, with a 'head of department' team responsible for the administration of their department.

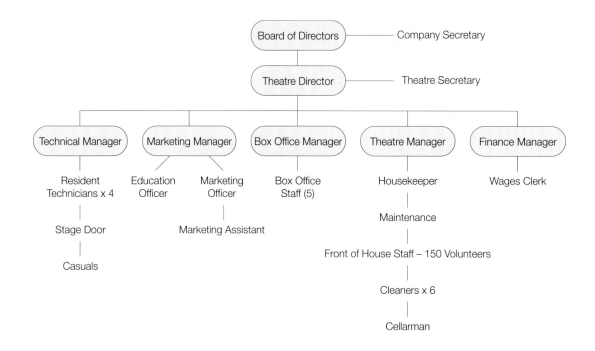

The following table indicates estimated expenditure for a hypothetical 1000-seat touring theatre.

Fixed Expenditure

Wages and Salaries

Administration	74,000	
Marketing and sales	104,640	
Stage	68,000	
House and catering	137,250	
	383,890	
National insurance @ 10.45%	40,117	
Pension @ 5%	19,195	443,201

Occupancy

Rates (50% charity relief)	12,000	
Heat and light	28,800	
Insurance	16,800	
Cleaning materials	9600	
Repairs and renewals	12,000	79,200

Administration

Computer consumables	3000	
Postage and printing	3000	
Staff recruitment	2000	
Telephone	10,400	
Equipment hire	5000	
Audit/Accountancy	10,000	
Bank charges (including credit card commissions)	7000	
Entertaining	2500	
Office supplies	3500	
Late night staff taxis	1500	
Travel and subsistence	3000	
Depreciation	40,000	
Legal	2000	
Licences and subscriptions (inc. T.M.A.)	2500	95,400

Marketing

Marketing: theatre share, inc. press advertising	25,000	
Membership and other promotion	5000	
Postage and distribution	15,000	
Season brochures	60,000	105,000

Education and Outreach

Schools packs, etc	10,000	10,000

Stage

Stage, sound and lighting supplies	12,000	12,000

ADD: Contingency @ 5% (excluding wages)		15,080

Total Expenditure	**£759,881**
Weekly Theatre Overheads	**£14,613**

The theatre aims to recover its weekly overheads (which can reach £40,000 in the biggest independently managed lyric theatres) from the theatre's box-office share and other earned income such as the net profit on bars, catering, programmes, merchandising, sponsorship and Friends' membership schemes. A 1000-seat theatre might expect to make about £4000 net profit per week from ancillary income, leaving a target in excess of £10,000 per week to retain at the box office. If this annual margin for the theatre averages twenty per cent, the weekly box-office receipts would need to average £50,000 net of VAT.

Ticket prices preoccupy the organisation: these may reflect the production's cost, are variable to suit the zone of the auditorium, the artform and, often, the individual production. Pricing (and discounting with concessions or special offers) is a sophisticated aspect of theatre marketing: charging what the market will bear is easier said than done! The income for this hypothetical 1000-seat theatre might breakdown as follows:

Anual Income and Expenditure

Box-office receipts: 48 playing weeks – average 55% attendance x 288 performances (158,400 theatregoers; 550 paying theatregoers at each performance) x £9.50 ticket yield (net of VAT)		£1,504,800
LESS Production Company Share		1,203,840
RETAINED by Theatre (annual margin of 20%)		300,960
ADD Other Earned Income		
Bars (62% margin)	92,000	
Ices (50% margin)	30,000	
Soft drinks (64% margin)	2000	
Programmes (67% margin)	23,000	
Cafe (35% margin)	10,000	
Sweets (31% margin)	4000	
Merchandising: facility fees	6000	
Room hires	1500	
Sponsorship and corporate memberships	25,000	
Friends of the Theatre	8000	
Kiosk rental	5000	
TOTAL Ancillary profit (£1.30 per theatregoer)		206,500
Total Earned Income		**£507,460**
Less Expenditure		759,881
Net Operating Loss		**£252,421**

We have reached the bottom line: whatever the annual loss in the commercial operation of a touring theatre, arguments for subsidy have to be made to government. Much material is published on this subject and the producing theatre companies are generally more experienced advocates. We must tell the government what the theatre can do for them not what they ought to do for the theatre. A new accountability is being demanded, to stakeholders and the communities served by theatres. In addition to un-fashionable polemic about the art of the theatre, grants are now justified by every conceivable robust reason – as good for business, cultural diversity, international profile, tourism, the creative economy, education, social inclusion, employment, reducing crime, urban or rural regeneration and national or regional identity. Theatres are judged as one element of the 'cultural industries'. Partnerships and collaborations with the community and with government are as important for a theatre as are those with artists and theatre makers.

Conclusion

Art isn't easy
Even when you're hot
Advancing art is easy
Financing it is not.

– Stephen Sondheim, 'Putting it Together',
Sunday in the Park with George, 1984

The fascinating thing about theatre management is that nothing is certain. There are few rules and no magic bullet. Week by week, year by year, the unexpected is constantly turning up. Whether it is favourable or the reverse depends very much on *luck*. Luck is probably the most important influence that anybody connected with theatre management must have. Luck, and a sense of dedication, or put less high falutingly, a complete and absorbing interest in the theatre to the exclusion of everything else. To run a theatre successfully needs much clear thinking, patience and forbearance on the part of the board and the manager. It also calls for great care and flair in programme build-ing so as to achieve balance and a consistent standard. This breeds confidence. It is futile to present shows to rows of empty seats. It is also wrong to think of what we do as some kind of social duty. We must remember that it can all be great fun too – an alluring adventure of unlimited variety and multiplicity of detail.

THE THEATRICAL MANAGER.

1 Managers in producing theatres often describe touring theatres as 'receiving' theatres or 'venues'. This tension began when Miss Horniman, founder of the repertory movement at the Gaiety Theatre Manchester, had to disband her permanent company in 1917. She described the Gaiety's new touring role as being a 'lodging house theatre', for she was in no way responsible for the companies that played there. The Arts Councils now prefer to describe the best of these as 'presenting' theatres, where the manager insists on reading all plays or seeing attractions before they visit, networking in the creative side of the business.

2 Theatres (and pay for artists) were graded according to size and reputation. All Moss' Empires and Howard and Wyndham theatres were No. 1 (such as the Theatres Royal Newcastle upon Tyne, Nottingham and Glasgow). A No. 2 theatre was usually smaller and often located in a seaside resort (such as the Gaiety Theatre, Ayr and the Royal Opera House, Scarborough), a spa town (Buxton Opera House) or small industrial town (such as Wakefield Theatre Royal and Opera House or Doncaster Grand Theatre). No. 3 theatres were located in market towns or suburbs (these often had fetching names, such as the Dalrymple Theatre Fraserburgh, the Theatre De Luxe Keighley and the Bostock and Wombwell Royal Italian Menagerie and Opera House). Today there are still different circuits of different sizes of theatre.

3 This company was forerunner to Stoll Moss Theatres Limited, now principally a London West End theatre owner. Its Profit and Loss Account for the year ending 31 December 1997 shows a profit of £6,531,000 before tax, on a turnover of £73,349,000.

4 Apollo Leisure Group plc. The Group Profit and Loss Account for the year ending 29 November 1997 shows a profit of £5,131,908 before tax, on a turnover of £95,038,447 (1996: £6,026,536 profit on a turnover of £64,484,303). This company owns or manages twenty-five theatres, often in partnership with local authorities. It has additional independent ticketing and cinema interests and, in 1997, moved into the sport and recreation business. When founded in 1977, it set its ambition against what seemed an inexorable decline in touring theatres and has become the new colossus of the circuit: in only twenty-one years it has created the second biggest theatre group in the world.

5 Examples of companies occupying a core role at a touring theatre include Birmingham Royal Ballet at the Birmingham Hippodrome, Welsh National Opera at the Cardiff New Theatre, Scottish Opera at the Theatre Royal Glasgow, Opera North at Leeds Grand Theatre, Théâtre sans Frontières at the Queen's Hall, Hexham, the D'Oyly Carte Opera Company at the Grand Theatre, Wolverhampton.

6 For example, Belfast Grand Opera House Trust, which manages this 1001-seat restored Frank Matcham touring theatre, gave 371 performances in the year ending 31 March 1997, selling a remarkable seventy-four per cent of capacity (275,000 theatregoers). It made a surplus of £22,169 on a turnover of £2,864,372, but received a grant of £590,000 from the Arts Council of Northern Ireland.

7 Mayflower Theatre Trust Limited, Report and Accounts 31 March 1997. This 2299-seat theatre gave 346 performances, selling 460,000 tickets with a turnover of £6.9 million. Included in revenue was ancillary profits from bars, catering and merchandise of £495,000.

8 The Birmingham Hippodrome Theatre Trust Limited, Report and Accounts 31 March 1996. This 1887-seat theatre had a turnover of £8.5 million. Year on year trading conditions fluctuate: in 1997 this theatre turned over £7.7 million and made a small loss of £99,519.

9 I am indebted to Robert Cogo-Fawcett and Crispin Raymond, former managers of the Theatre Royal, Bath for assistance with contract explanations. A fuller explanation is offered by Raymond in 'Deal Structures', appendix two in *Once More with Feeling!* Arts Council of England, London, 1998.

10 Research into local authority subsidy levels in touring theatres was last undertaken by Crispin Raymond in 1992, when he found that middle-scale theatres (average capacity 540 seats) run by local authorities cost between two and three times more in subsidy than those run by independent trusts.

11 High Peak Theatre Trust Limited operates this Edwardian theatre for its historic value and its contemporary use; it had a turnover of £1.1 million in the year ending 31 March 1998, making a surplus of £23,609 after subsidy from the local authority of £43,050. The Opera House occupies a strong role in a small town at the centre of a large rural area (there are only 87,000 people in the immediate catchment), attracting an average of 416 paying theatregoers at each performance.

12 See John McGrath, *A Good Night Out*, Methuen, London, 1981, pp. 77–82.

Grand Theatre, Blackpool

'The battle for its survival was one of the earliest of a series of events which eventually turned the tide of post-War destruction of theatres'

(*Curtains!!!* New edition)

Introduction

Almost everyone in Blackpool knows the *Grand Theatre*. Its domed and canopied exterior occupies a prominent site right in the centre of the main shopping area. The bars and café are open all day, and at the beginning of each season Blackpool's small army of landladies and taxi drivers are invited to preview the summer show, which will run until the illuminations are turned off. For the rest of the year, the local residents are presented with a rich programme of drama, music (popular and classical), comedy, dance, opera, musicals, children's productions, studio productions and workshops and the occasional show on ice.

The theatre is also known because it has one of the most energetic and well-established group of 'Friends' in the country. Just over twenty-five years ago they campaigned, raised funds and held midnight concerts to get the theatre reopened and then, paintbrushes in hand, set about renovating the building. The *Grand Theatre* belongs to them, in every sense of the word.

It opened in 1894, designed by Frank Matcham, the most prolific and respected theatre architect of the period, who was responsible for five theatres in Blackpool alone. The *Grand* is considered to be one of his finest buildings. In the centenary appeal brochure, Samuel Lee, chairman of the Blackpool Grand Theatre Trust Ltd, wrote, 'We appeal to you to help us save and protect Lancashire's liveliest and loveliest public building for our own time and for the theatregoers of the future. This splendid building is an extraordinary example of outstanding architectural design provided for ordinary people. It is a source of pride for the people of Lancashire and it is our duty to cherish it for those who will follow us.'

The threat to survival

By the time the theatre reached its first centenary, there were good reasons for celebration but some earlier birthdays were far less happy occasions. The 1960s saw the growth of the 'package deal' holiday, and with it the decline of the seaside visit and the audience for Britain's resort theatres. The *Blackpool Grand* appeared to be nearing the end of its life. In the summer of 1972, a notice was fixed to the theatre's door stating that permission to demolish the theatre was being sought by the owners (then the Blackpool Tower Company with its parent company EMI) together with Littlewoods Stores Ltd and the Blackpool Corporation. A joint application was made to clear the space for 'improvements' to regenerate the area – the run-down theatre would be replaced by a smart new Littlewoods' department store. It is ironic that twenty-five years on, the theatre is thriving while the store which was to replace it is closing its outlets throughout the country.

The 'rescue' bid

The application for demolition served to ignite support for the theatre. Retired banker, Burt Briggs, launched the rescue bid from the steps of the *Grand* holding up a protest petition signed by 10,000 people. The local press and media backed the campaign and over 300 people attended the public meeting when the case for the preservation of the theatre was formally presented. As a result of all this activity, the application was called in by the Department of the Environment and a planning inquiry held. By then the Friends had secured the theatre its grade II★ listing. The planning inquiry dismissed the application and the immediate threat to the building was averted (August 1973). The Blackpool Grand Theatre Trust Ltd was formed, with Burt

Briggs in the chair, and a professionally managed campaign and appeal was launched to raise the purchase price for the theatre. The asking price was £350,000.

Bingo!

While the demolition had been stopped, the theatre was far from being 'saved'. The position was initially one of deadlock, with the owners stuck with a run-down and loss-making old theatre and the trust faced with the problem of not only getting sufficient money to buy the building but of being able to afford to renovate the interior and run the whole operation.

Continuing discussions led to a solution of sorts. The trust agreed to give public support to EMI's application for a bingo licence and in return won the company's agreement to:

- restore the *Grand Theatre* under the guidance of a theatre consultant (John Wyckham, the Friends' choice, was appointed);
- the right of the trust to present, for the first two weeks after the restoration was completed and before the bingo operation began, live theatre (at a rent of £1000 per week);
- the right to present on ten occasions each year (except two months in the summer) shows at times to be chosen by the Friends of the theatre at times of days which did not conflict with bingo and on a twelve-feet depth of stage (all that would be available once the bingo apparatus was installed) at a cost rent (then £100 per show);
- the option to buy the theatre – excluding the shops – for a price of £350,000 or market value at the time of the option if higher, at any time within the twenty years commencing 1 October 1978 (when the bingo lease expired) – although giving EMI sufficient time to relocate their bingo club.

This must have been a hard decision to make at the time but demonstrated a realism of approach which was to prove crucial to the longer-term success of the project. The bingo interlude served to strengthen the trust's position by 'buying time' and, eventually, by securing for them a building which had already been substantially refurbished.

Protecting the theatre use

Although bingo has been the saviour of many Victorian and Edwardian theatres (by keeping the buildings open and maintained), the demands of commercial bingo on the scale

The Baroque corner entrance has changed little in 100 years.
(*photo right, Ian Grundy*)

required for *Blackpool Grand* were not readily compatible with the needs of a live performance venue. The bingo operation required 'unit seating' (tables and banquettes) in the stalls all at right angles to the stage and on the stage itself; indicator boards at a position which limited the stage depth; equipment filling much of the wing space; and a fully carpeted stage housing a 'blower' mechanism. Correspondence on The Theatres Trust's files reveals that protracted discussions were held with EMI to try to lessen the impact of their operation on the interior of the building.

In addition to these physical constraints, the 'Bingo Boys' (as they were referred to by Friends) were adamant that for them to not open for bingo even for one day, would play havoc with their operation and they would lose their customers to a rival hall. The Friends had secured an agreement allowing them to mount ten shows a year but its terms meant that these shows had to be held either very early in the morning or after bingo closed at 10.30 p.m. While such a requirement would put off many a would-be impresario, the Friends proceeded to promote a series of midnight events. By keeping a live performance presence going in such difficult conditions, they were able to demonstrate the strength of local support for a theatre use.

Equally importantly, EMI honoured its agreement to redecorate the theatre (and by so doing strengthened the case for its retention). A letter from the Friends to The Theatres Trust in 1977 describes the theatre as having recently been 'completely redecorated, restoring it to its previous brilliance'. The Friends were also allowed to open an appeal office within the building.

Reversal of fortunes

By the middle of 1979, while the Friends were well on their way to raising their interim target of £100,000, the bingo operation was rumoured to be heading into trouble – attendance levels were so low that the income no longer covered the running costs. Blackpool Corporation had by then been won over to the Friends' cause and was actively supporting their bid to secure the *Grand* for live performance.

At a reception attended by Norman St. John Stevas (then Minister for Arts) in October 1979, EMI and the Friends issued a joint statement – the asking price for the theatre had been reduced to £250,000 and Blackpool Corporation, anxious to see the theatre open for the next summer season, had agreed to contribute £50,000 from its local lottery fund and make a loan of a further £50,000 repayable over the following three years.

'We're back!!'

Fundraising continued while studies were carried out to establish what work had to be done before the theatre could once again become operational on a regular basis. The trust found that it needed to refurbish the stage, backstage and gallery; to reinstall lighting and sound systems; and to provide for extra box-office facilities. It was optimistic about reaching the new target figure – 'money is rolling in now'. Exactly one year after the joint announcement, a celebration party was held to mark the formal acquisition of the *Grand Theatre* by the trust.

Advertisements were placed in the press announcing that 'Britain's Finest Theatre is available for First Class Shows from Spring 1981'. Companies interested in easter and summer season, pantomime and touring productions were invited to apply. The *Grand Theatre* reopened in March 1981 with a performance of *The Merchant of Venice* (starring Timothy West and Prunella Scales) and held a royal gala performance in May of that year in the presence of the Prince of Wales.

Live theatre was back at the *Grand* after an interim of nearly ten years and the trust had started out on the long and continuing task of ensuring that it stayed that way.

Running the theatre

The trust set out to build on the support generated during its long campaign and provide live entertainment for a wide range of people. During the first few years of its operation it succeeded in putting the *Grand* back on the map for first-class touring products of all kinds. It was supported in this by the Arts Council's touring department which encouraged both the Old Vic and English National Opera North to visit in its opening year. Press coverage at the time expresses both surprise and satisfaction that Shakespeare and opera could attract almost capacity audiences in Blackpool. The trust saw it as justifying its claim that there had long been an unsatisfied need for good quality live theatre to be available for the area.

The trust also set out to restore the role of the *Grand* as a key provider of live entertainment for Blackpool's holiday-makers, putting on a spring festival and a season of summer shows.

As a community theatre, it saw one of its roles as that of introducing children to live performance both through work with schools and special children's shows. A 'Young Friends of the Grand Society' was created to encourage younger audiences. The *Grand* also became a 'home' for many of the thriving amateur companies already established in the area and for the Fylde Arts Association, providing a meeting place for people of all ages with an interest in the arts.

Establishing viability

Prior to 1981 most of the trust's energies and all of its money had gone into the purchase of the theatre and the renewal of the equipment needed to operate it. It had also been faced with the difficult task of appointing staff, getting a full programme off the ground at very short notice, attracting audiences back to the venue and raising sufficient income to cover its costs. Hardly surprisingly, it failed to meet its targets during the first year of its operation (incurring losses of £127,000). During the second year it was able to realise a small profit but by the third year the *Grand* was again in deficit.

By the end of 1984, the trust was forced to recognise that, even with careful management and good audiences, the theatre could not, at that time, be run on a self-financing basis. It needed an immediate injection of £100,000 to avoid possible receivership and regular subsidy to maintain its operation. Its researches identified that only six out of the 115 regional theatres operating at that time were self-sufficient and that many were receiving subsidies far in excess of the amount needed by the *Grand*.

Market analyses demonstrated that audiences were drawn from the surrounding areas as follows:

40 per cent Blackpool Borough Council area
30 per cent Wyre Borough Council area
30 per cent Fylde Borough Council area.

(*Ian Grundy*)

The difficulty of obtaining a trading profit in an obviously successful theatre is a difficult concept for the public to grasp. They have seen packed houses during the summer and at various times during the year. They do not appreciate the extremely high cost of staging a professional product in a theatre, e.g. for the Les Dawson Show, despite extremely hard bargaining, the *Grand Theatre* had to accept a share of only 27.5 per cent of the net box-office receipts, i.e. the receipts after the deduction of 15 per cent VAT, the balance going to the producing company.'

Once revenue support had been secured, the *Grand Theatre* began to establish itself as a viable operation. Since 1985, it has continued to aim at self-sufficiency and has achieved this objective more often than not.

By the tenth anniversary, in 1991, the *Grand* had achieved three consecutive years of record ticket sales. During the previous year, 280,000 tickets were sold and the turnover had reached £2 million. Its success continued to surprise some commentators. Stephen Pile, writing in *The Daily Telegraph* (9 June 1993), describes the achievements of the theatre under the heading 'Kiss me quick, the opera's on' and begins the article 'No, don't laugh, the *Grand Theatre* in Blackpool is packing them in with Handel, Shakespeare and lesbian drama … furthermore, the *Grand* has become the centre for the very latest modern dance'. He goes on to explain 'a unique set of conditions' which makes the programming mix possible. 'First, when all other theatres go quiet during the summer, the *Grand* sets up a money-making show for holidaymakers that helps fund the rest of the programme. The policy of the *Grand* is that everything counts as culture.'

The *Grand* had established that the summer show held the key to its financial viability and soon boasted the longest summer season in the country – twenty weeks at one point. But as the only major touring theatre between Manchester and Glasgow, *Blackpool Grand* was also able to draw audiences throughout the rest of the year from Cumbria, Lancashire and even West Yorkshire to support its drama, dance and opera programme. It was helped by the continuing support of its Friends. By its tenth anniversary it had established a worldwide support group totalling 2500 people. Two hundred of these were prepared to work on a voluntary basis to a rota system providing ushers and front-of-house services, saving the theatre an estimated £35,000 a year in salaries. (The *Grand* now claims a Friends organisation of over 3000.)

At the end of 1993 the management board was divided into two, with an Arts and Entertainment Board looking after the programme and activities, and a Grand Theatre Trust Board

The trust put together a case for financial support based on the achievements of the previous three years and approached these Councils (and the County authority) for support, hoping that each would contribute an amount proportional to its residents' attendances. The result was that Blackpool Corporation agreed to provide £100,000 for the year 1985/86; Lancashire County Council gave £10,000, while Wyre and Fylde Councils declined to make any contribution. Most importantly, Blackpool Corporation agreed to underwrite future deficits.

A report entitled 'Trading History' which the trust produced in 1985, explains the problems it had encountered.

The problem of limited front-of-house space was tackled, in part, by the creation of Matcham Court, a covered courtyard to the rear of the theatre. (*Ian Grundy*)

taking responsibility for the building. This was done to ensure that the theatre would survive any unforeseen problems which the production side might incur.

Improvements, adaptations and renewals

Although the Blackpool *Grand* had virtually ceased operating as a theatre for nearly ten years, the building itself never closed. It reached its lowest ebb some thirty years ago when its deteriorating fabric led to the 'eyesore' status which made some think it a worthy target for demolition. Since 1971 a regular and continuing input of capital (first by EMI and then by the trust) not only ensured the survival of the building but gave it the reputation of being one of the most immaculate Victorian theatres in the country.

Improvements have been made over the years but no major restructuring of the auditorium, stage, backstage or front of house has been undertaken. The whole theatre is very much as Matcham designed it. While this creates some operational problems (a tight entrance foyer, circuitous circulation routes and a difficult backstage get-in), it gives the theatre a very special quality.

Initially, the trust concentrated on ensuring that the structure itself was in good condition. Even this was a struggle. Having agreed to purchase the building, the trust had immediately to find another £100,000 to get the theatre operational. In 1984, the trust reported, 'As the theatre has been forced to live a hand to mouth existence, all donations, etc. have been swallowed up by the day to day requirements and the bare minimum has been spent on repairs and renewals.'

The money for the first bit of work to be done to the exterior came by chance. EMI had installed a plastic canopy and facia board over the entrance to the building to announce the fact that it was a bingo hall. Though the letters had been removed, the structure remained until it was largely blown down in a storm. The insurance money helped pay for a replacement 'more in keeping with the quality of the building'. That same year, the trust had to find another £50,000 to tackle a list of small repairs which were needed to maintain the fabric of the building.

The theatre had contained a 'kiosk' (a small shop) which the trust had refurbished and let. The income from this had helped pay for some of the capital work. In September 1986, listed building consent was given for five more kiosks to be inserted into the theatre structure where it abutted the street. Though this development resulted in the loss of some sixteen seats at the back of the stalls ('the least attractive in the house') it produced a regular source of income for the theatre which more than compensated for the small reduction in seating capacity. The design of the development was considered to have enhanced the Church Street frontage, being 'an elegant feature, reminiscent of the iron and glass queue canopy which must have originally existed'.

By 1990 it was evident that additional work was required to maintain the structure of the building. The brick and carved stonework of the exterior was being badly eroded 'caused by salt air over ninety-six years'. There was sufficient in the building renovation fund (money accumulated from the kiosk rentals over the previous four years) to cover the £60,000 cost of this work.

Blackpool Grand was one of the theatres which benefited from the short-lived Theatres Restoration Fund, set up by the Government in April 1991 in association with the Wolfson Foundation and Family Charitable Trust. One of the first thirteen grants announced (December 1992), the *Grand* was awarded £150,000. This was matched by a similar amount of the

(*Photogenics*)

theatre's own money to finance the renovation of the Victorian theatre annex to provide new backstage facilities, including a rehearsal room and dressing-rooms, both with disabled access. As well as providing much needed facilities for the theatre operation, the new spaces brought in additional income from lets.

The *Grand* has also improved its café/bars over the years, the most recent project being the major refurbishment of the Matcham bar. This was part of an Arts Council lottery backed package of capital expenditure which included work to improve access, upgrade safety installations, renovate the heating and ventilation system, refurbish the gallery area, and enhance the area to the back of the theatre. The pub-style Matcham bar opens onto what is now a covered courtyard, with its new glazed roofing supported by brightly painted and decoratively wrought columns. Before the lottery award, this was a dingy backyard.

The gallery presents the theatre with a dilemma. It accommodates 300 people but seats them on the traditional benches. Reseating the area would provide more comfort but it would also reduce the 1200-plus seating capacity which gives the theatre the status it needs to attract good product. These seats still sell well for the summer show but the manager has noticed that it is now mainly the older members of the audience who are prepared to climb the many steps (passing the 'Halfway' notice installed to encourage the despairing) to sit on the benches. This time round the trust has opted to cushion and recover the benches rather than reseat the area.

Accessibility also presents problems. The theatre has its entrance and foyer in a baroque style cornerpiece giving straight onto the pavement. The rest of the site at ground level is occupied either by the auditorium or by shops which, though originally owned by the theatre, had been sold off at some stage in its history. The routes from the small entrance foyer to the theatre bars and to the toilets go along narrow corridors, round tight corners and up and down small flights of steps. Those who have problems in getting around have easy access to the newly refurbished Matcham bar and to the rehearsal/studio space but experience more difficulty elsewhere in the building. Wheel-chairs can, however, be manoeuvred into the auditorium through a door at the back of the stalls which, fortuitously, opens direct (and without change of level) onto the outside pavement.

In the longer term, the theatre hopes to be able to undertake further work to extend its foyer spaces and improve the accessibility and circulation routes.

The current operation

The *Grand* continues to develop its programme in line with the successful pattern which it established during the earlier years. The summer show (seventeen weeks this year) and the panto-mime continue to be its financial linchpins, enabling the general manager to bring in good quality productions, including some more experimental work, during the rest of the year. For the spring 1988 season, the *Grand* was showing West End hits and touring drama productions; musicals and light opera by pro-fessional companies and by local groups; comedy shows; personal appearances; orchestral evenings; and dance productions from a range of established companies. The main programme is now supplemented by smaller-scale work, theatre in education pro-ductions, and comedy in the studio/rehearsal space.

Young people's and children's theatre remain a very strong element of its programme with shows put on both for and by this age group. The theatre maintains good working relationships with the local schools which respond by bringing large groups of children to the daytime (including some morning) productions. Successive generations of local children are told about the theatre's history and its importance to the town.

The theatre retains some of its 'bucket shaking' approach to fundraising and Friends still take on front-of-house jobs on a voluntary basis but the whole operation is now far less dependent on these goodwill gestures than it was originally. The 1996 accounts show that the theatre was turning over £2,051,146 and showing an operational profit of £85,619 (of which £40,000 was appropriated to the programming reserve fund to support potential losses in the future). These figures included £55,716 of covenanted income but no subsidies from public funds. The theatre also benefits from sponsorship, particularly for its

Education for all programme and its studio productions. Income from this source is accounted for within the figures for the production to which it relates. (These figures were taken from the audited accounts for the year ended 26 October 1996.)

1998 marks the twenty-fifth anniversary season for the *Grand Theatre* (if the seasons during the bingo years are included). As the Friends celebrate this achievement, the theatre presents a programme which is as stimulating and varied as you could find anywhere in the country. While some other middle-scale theatres outside the major cities are facing problems, *Blackpool Grand* seems to have worked out its strategies for survival and looks well set for a good, long run.

Key Points

- A seaside resort theatre which appeared to have reached the end of its natural life
- Local enthusiasts got it listed and opposed an application for its demolition
- An agreement with owner EMI secured the refurbishment of the building
- A 'Friends' group set up a trust and raised the money to buy the building
- The theatre is now virtually self-sufficient
- Its programme is designed to appeal to everybody living in or visiting the area

Type of operation:
Receiving venue with long summer show
Ownership and management:
Owned and managed by Blackpool Grand Theatre Trust Ltd
Original architect:
Frank Matcham 1894
Subsequent architects:
1980 onwards MacKeith Dickinson & Partners
Listed:
Grade II*
Uses:

1894–1972	*theatre*
1972–80	*bingo with occasional live performances*
1981 continuing	*theatre*

Current capacity:
Main auditorium 1215 Studio 80

The city council were so determined to safeguard the future of this building that they were prepared to buy it to stop it being turned into a Bingo Club … and buy it they did.

Introduction

First the *Empire*, then the *Gaumont*, now the *Mayflower* – all the same building but each name representing a different period in its history. The building opened in December 1928 as the *Empire Variety Theatre*, designed by theatre architects W and T R Milburn. It was the last theatre to be built as part of the Moss Empire circuit. It enjoyed just over a decade of full-time live entertainment until the outbreak of World War II when it was taken over by the War Department. Like many other theatres at the time, its proscenium arch was screened over and for the next few years its key role was to show films to the troops passing through the busy terminus of Southampton Docks. In 1941 the building was purchased by Gaumont British Picture Corporation and renamed the *Gaumont*.

After the war the building continued to be run predominantly as a cinema but with some live performances. The balance changed during the 1960s when the *Gaumont* became known as a major venue on the pop and rock band circuit. By the end of the next decade, the Arts Council had added the theatre to its list of major venues for the large-scale ballet and opera company tours. But it became increasingly evident that things would have to change. The cinema use was proving unviable and the band circuit had moved on to larger venues. The owners (by then called Rank Theatres Ltd) sought to close the cinema/theatre operation and reopen the building as a bingo club.

This case study looks at how Southampton City Council fought the planning battle to retain the theatre and then turned it from a potential 'white elephant' into one of the country's most commercially successful operations.

The planning applications

The building had been listed grade II which meant that Rank required listed building consent for the internal alterations required for bingo, as well as planning permission for 'change of use' and an operating licence. Rank made an attempt to secure 'change of use' permission in June 1970 but withdrew the application after discussions with the city council. Towards the end of 1980, reports once again began to appear in the local press about Rank's plans for the future of the building. A new application was submitted in March 1981 and, in accordance with legislative requirements, was referred to The Theatres Trust in London for comment. The Trust wrote that it would recommend the rejection of any application which 'would deprive the City and neighbourhood of the type of productions now seen at the *Gaumont*, or would destroy the theatrical character of the building'. Similar opposition came from the Arts Council's touring department and from Southern Arts. Southampton City Council identified five alternative sites within the central area where a bingo house would be accepted. Faced with this united opposition, Rank once again withdrew the application and, for a while, the programme of mixed cinema and live performance continued. A reprieve had been granted but the problem of running a loss-making venue had certainly not been solved.

Rank tries again

Within the year, Rank resubmitted its application for change of use and this time backed it with an application to the Justices of the Peace for a bingo club licence (April 1982). Opposition to the proposal had strengthened during the preceding months and the planning committee received 126 individual letters and petitions signed by around 4000 signatories. The applications went through the same processes and received the same response – refusals. The chief executive of Southampton City Council set out his council's position in a letter to The Theatres Trust. 'The council are determined to safeguard the future of the *Gaumont Theatre* in so far as it lies within their power and are certainly prepared to buy it to avoid the use of the *Gaumont* for bingo.'

Rank was in a difficult position. It could not run a profitable theatre/cinema operation nor could it use the building for other purposes. In December 1982, it lodged an appeal. The Department of the Environment called in the application and a public local inquiry was set up.

Support rallied to the city council in its determination to maintain the *Gaumont* as a venue for live entertainment. Objections were registered by the Arts Council of Great Britain; The Theatres Trust; the Theatres Advisory Council; Southampton Theatre Guild; Southampton Musical Society; Glyndebourne Festival Opera; Friends of Welsh National Opera; the Leisure Consultative Committee and Hampshire County Council. Over one hundred names (individuals or representatives of different interest groups) joined the list of consultees.

The case for the theatre

The Inquiry was held on 15 November 1983, with Mr J P MacBryde RIBA, MRTPI, MCIT, FRSA appointed as the inspector. His report recommended that the appeal be dismissed on the grounds that 'planning permission for the building's change of use would be against the public interest since there is every prospect of the existing theatre use being perpetuated'. The following points were noted:

- the *Gaumont* had a vital role for a sizeable proportion of the population living within the London, Southampton, Bristol triangle which could not be matched by any other existing theatres within the area;
- the building was 'functionally adequate' for its role as a theatre (especially as there was scope for improvements to be made);
- the existing use was in line with the 'relevant emergent provisions of both Structure and Local Plans';
- the special architectural or historic interest of the *Gaumont Theatre* would be best preserved by a continuation of its use as a theatre;
- there was every prospect of the *Gaumont* continuing its theatre use (as distinct from cinema use which he saw as 'nationally in steep decline');

- there was clear evidence of overwhelming support for the retention of the *Gaumont* as a place for live entertainment.

As a result of this decision, Rank got the city council to agree to underwrite the losses which they were likely to incur 'to secure live show content during the period 1 July 1984 and 30 June 1985' and to open negotiations for the purchase of the building. The city sought advice as to its value and, in November 1985, bought the *Gaumont* for the sum of £650,000. As part of the deal, the Rank organisation was appointed to manage the refurbishment project (for a fee of £350,000).

Fifteen years after the first, tentative application to close the cinema/theatre, Rank's problems were solved. Southampton City Council had acquired the 2000-seat-plus theatre (the fourth

largest in the UK) but with only a few weeks of Arts Council-backed touring product to pull the audiences in.

Not surprisingly, there were those who thought the council had bought itself a whole heap of trouble.

Changing course

The building was already nearly sixty years old and, with its poor turnover and the questions hanging over its future, had not been well maintained. The first job which faced the new owners was to refurbish and improve the building. The city council set up Southampton City Leisure Limited (an arm of the local authority) to plan and run a capital works programme. Dennis Hall was appointed theatre director. He had worked for many years in the management of Bournemouth Corporation's theatres, which included the *Bournemouth International Centre*, a 4000-seat conference/entertainment venue.

In 1986 the building closed so that the refurbishment work could start. The project involved a complete restoration of the auditorium; the addition of a new scene dock and improved workshop and get-in; the enlargement of the bars; and the modernisation of the box-office and front-of-house provision. The seating in the auditorium was completely replaced, increasing the capacity to 2300 (plus 130 standing). Part of the standing area was converted to take wheelchairs, and facilities for people with disabilities were improved. Major improvements were made to the backstage areas and to the technical equipment. Video screens were installed to link the different parts of the theatre and technically advanced sound and lighting equipment connected to a new computer controlled operations centre. The architects for the refurbishment work were Weguelin Yearly.

The bulk of the £4 million cost was borne by the city council with a grant of £500,000 coming from the Arts Council's Housing the Arts Fund (one of the last before the fund closed).

The Mayflower is launched

In February 1987, the old *Gaumont* reopened as the *Mayflower Theatre* and set out to fulfil the aspirations of those who had fought for its survival. An independent trust, The Mayflower Theatre Trust Ltd, was formed to manage both the theatre operation and the building. The city council gave it a 125-year lease.

Dennis Hall's aim was to be independent, avoiding the restrictions which came from being financed from the local authority purse. He knew he had a large space to fill, not just during the opening weeks or on special occasions, but week by

week and year on year. To succeed in the long term, the theatre had to establish itself right at the outset and he secured an undertaking from the city council to provide £1 million to support the programme during the first three years, enabling him to buy into the market at the appropriate level. In the event the operation needed £350,000 during the first year; with £150,000 in the second and £275,000 in the third. By the end of 1991, the trust was able to announce that it was in profit – 'an exceptional year for shows, but it was the culmination of three year's groundwork'. For several years the *Mayflower* continued to receive a subsidy of £55,000–£60,000, income regarded as contributing to the renewal and maintenance budget rather than to programme support. The subsidy ceased in 1996/97.

The *Mayflower* is open throughout the year (closing only when bringing in large-scale new productions). It mounts nearly 400 performances a year and attracts annual audiences of 430,000–500,000; achieving average capacities of sixty-six to seventy per cent. The 1997/98 turnover of £7 million is expected to increase to £8 million in 1998/99.

How has this been achieved?

The *Mayflower* has both a large seating capacity and a large catchment area but these are only advantages if the potential audiences can be attracted into the theatre. Dennis Hall set out to establish

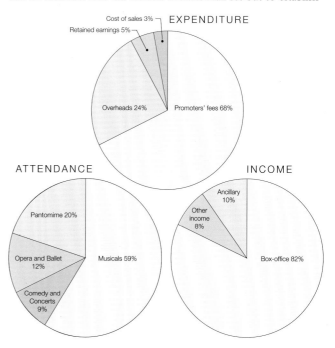

a programme of sufficient variety to draw in people of all age groups and all tastes and of sufficient quality to encourage people to travel. Southampton and its environs are relatively poor but the area from which the wider audience is drawn – the south coast resorts and home counties commuter land – is an affluent one. As the national ballet and opera company visits and the large-scale musicals tended to be targeted at this wider audience, the decision was taken to price them accordingly (comparable with other large cities but about half that charged by the West End theatres).

The *Mayflower* now has a database of 150,000 and a strong marketing team. Its large audiences help to secure good quality productions. The *Mayflower* also increased its negotiating strength by establishing links with other major touring theatres. In 1996/97, for example, the theatre was able to secure the final date of the tour of *Joseph and the Amazing Technicolor Dreamcoat* starring Philip Schofield, which played the theatre for seven weeks from 24 April 1996. The production attracted 112,000 people and alone accounted for twenty-nine per cent of the box-office sales for the year.

A strategy which proved successful was that of establishing the *Mayflower* as a top corporate entertainment venue for the area – with quality product and good catering helping to bring corporate clients on board. This led to an increase in sponsorship.

The theatre has set up its own trading company which handles all the commercial aspects of the theatre operation and has plans to extend the scope of its activities (e.g. organising group bookings for other events).

Maintaining and improving the building

During the ten years of its operation, the trust has allocated regular amounts of money to the maintenance budget and has raised additional money to carry out further work on the building. In 1994, the *Mayflower* launched an appeal to raise the £750,000 it needed for improvements to its customer facilities.

Though the theatre has the advantage of being only a few minutes walk from both the mainline station and the city centre and has good parking facilities, its immediate surroundings are somewhat run-down and these routes are uninviting. The city council (with a developer) is now planning to redevelop the area. If implemented, the scheme will provide additional office space for the theatre and extend the original stage and fly-tower (both are rather limited in the facilities they offer large-scale tours).

The plans include creating an 'Arts Square' with a new community arts centre linking into the theatre, and building on its success.

Notes on other theatres

The 'top five' venues for receiving large-scale musicals in England are the *Alhambra*, Bradford; the *Bristol Hippodrome*; the *Birmingham Hippodrome*; the *Mayflower* in Southampton and the two Apollo-owned Manchester theatres (the *Palace* and the *Opera House*) – plus the *Edinburgh Playhouse* in Scotland

W & T R Milburn's theatres (extant) include the *Empire Theatres* at Sunderland, Liverpool and Edinburgh (now the *Edinburgh Festival Theatre* – page 44), and the *Dominion* in London.

Key Points
- Large capacity auditorium, city centre site
- Used as a touring venue for Arts Council backed opera and dance productions
- Planning legislation used to fight closure as a live theatre
- Campaign spearheaded by the local authority and backed by national and regional arts and heritage interests
- Initial subsidy enabled the theatre to establish itself
- Now self-sufficient in revenue terms

Type of operation:
Receiving venue for large-scale touring productions
Ownership and management:
Owned by Southampton City Council and leased to the Mayflower Theatre Trust Ltd
Original architects:
1928 W and T R Milburn
Architects for 1986/87 refurbishment:
Weguelin Yearly
Listed:
Grade II
Uses:

1928–41	theatre (the Empire)
1941–86	cinema with some live performance (the Gaumont)
1987 continuing	theatre (the Mayflower)

Current capacity:
2300 (plus 130 standing)

'The proximity of the Lyceum to the Crucible, and the very differing styles of the two theatres, make a unique combination of opposites'

(RHWL's Design Report)

Introduction

The *Lyceum* Theatre occupies a prominent corner site in the centre of Sheffield, stretching along one side of what is now known as Tudor Square and close to the city's main library. Designed by the respected London theatre architect W G R Sprague, it opened in October 1897 with a production of Carmen by the Carl Rosa Company, followed by shows starring Sir Henry Irving and Ellen Terry. Throughout the early years of this century the *Lyceum* hosted a wide range of productions and established itself as an important touring venue. Its reputation continued to attract nationally known actors through to the 1960s, but by then the theatre had been starved of investment and lacked the comfort and amenities which audiences sought.

The *Lyceum* closed as a theatre in 1969, just two years before the *Crucible* opened next door. The new theatre, with its strong forms, bright colours, thrust stage and single rake of seats was regarded as the epitome of what contemporary theatre was all about. The *Lyceum*'s fast decaying Victorian splendour was seen as obsolete and the building was left for dead. Though the 1982 edition of *Curtains !!!* identified the *Lyceum* as one of its 'Sleeping Beauties' – theatres of exceptional quality which were lying unused and neglected – it saw little prospect of any early revival in its fortunes.

The campaign for the *Lyceum*'s reopening was a long fought battle which at times came very close to failure. In fact, it was only the alertness of the sympathetic management of the adjacent *Crucible* that stopped planning consent being given for alterations which, in the words of the Victorian Society, 'threatened to destroy any further hopes of the *Lyceum* ever reopening as a theatre'. While the ultimate success owes much to the determination of those who argued for the quality of the theatre building through decades of neglect, the turning point for the *Lyceum* came with an event quite unrelated to the theatrical life of the

city or even to the arts – when Sheffield decided to make a pitch for the World Student Games. Even then, with the strong support from Sheffield City Council, there were problems to be overcome as promised grants threatened to disappear into bureaucratic holes.

The *Lyceum* was eventually reopened in 1990. John Earl, then Director of The Theatres Trust, wrote, 'Happy is the word. The *Lyceum* is a spectacular success and the more exciting because it stood, dark and accusing, for altogether too long as a sad neighbour to the *Crucible*.'

The *Crucible* played a key role in the *Lyceum*'s revival. It was eventually recognised that the one theatre complemented the other – a proscenium partner to the *Crucible*'s thrust stage. Since 1991, the theatres have been run as a single organisation under the management of the Sheffield Theatres Trust, a company limited by guarantee and registered as a charity.

How the *Lyceum* went from a 'dark and accusing' spectre of the past to what is arguably the stronger partner of the Tudor Square theatres consortium is the subject of this study.

An example to be followed? The present *Lyceum* certainly shows what can be achieved but the story can also be read as a warning of how this fine theatre was so very nearly lost.

The dark years

The *Lyceum*'s history is recorded in a book produced by Sheffield Libraries to mark the reopening of the theatre. This relates how rumours about the *Lyceum*'s financial problems started as early as 1959 and that in 1961 the theatre closed for two months because of 'a shortage of attractions'. Two years later, Sheffield Corporation announced plans to demolish the building to make way for a new civic centre and from then on, any references to the theatre tended to be prefaced by the words *doomed* or *ailing*. Live

The *Crucible* (foreground) and the *Lyceum* (behind)
are run jointly by the Sheffield Theatres Trust. (*RHWL*)

performance gave way to bingo except for an annual pantomime.
The final curtain fell at the end of the pantomime run in March
1969 (though the bingo operation continued for a further three
years).

Two months later the first of many campaigns was launched.
It was led by the Sheffield amateur operatic and dramatic societies
and culminated in a petition being drawn up with 17,000 signatories calling for Sheffield City Council to take over the *Lyceum*
and run it as a civic enterprise. The cost of acquiring and refurbishing the theatre was then estimated to be £150,000.
No decision was made.

Interest was re-ignited in 1972 when the *Lyceum*'s imminent
closure was announced and plans for its demolition were put
in hand. It was at this point that a step was taken which was to
prove crucial to the *Lyceum*'s survival. The building had already
been recommended for preservation by the Hallamshire Historic
Building Society and, with demolition looking very much a
reality, the society urged the Department of the Environment
to make a decision. The theatre achieved grade II listed building status, mainly for the quality of its interior decoration and
plasterwork. The listing came as an immense relief to the
theatre's supporters but infuriated those with other plans who
described the campaigners as 'a group of meddling culture
vultures'. The group went on to form the Lyceum Theatre
Trust (Sheffield) Ltd.

When, in 1974, the formal application was made for the
building to be demolished, the issue went to public inquiry. The
Department of the Environment's inspector found in favour of
the campaigners, stating that the interior of the theatre 'deserves
every effort for it to be preserved for posterity' (April 1975).

Reports were commissioned both by the Arts Council
(Theatre Consultants John Wyckham Associates 1975) and by the
trust (Fry & Hughes Partnership 1976). The Wyckham report
drew attention to the disadvantages of the steeply raked gallery
and the small stage (thirty feet deep). It proposed extending the
stage by building onto the back of the theatre and converting
the gallery to form a studio theatre or arts cinema club, leaving
the main auditorium with a seating capacity of 800. (Estimated
cost £750,000 to £1 million.) The Fry and Hughes report
suggested the provision of a fore-stage and improvements to
the gallery, retaining the 1000 seats (though with poor sightlines
from the gallery to the fore-stage). The cost was estimated at
£400,000. The minimum cost for reinstatement 'as is' was
given as £200,000 'with strong reservations'.

Once again the prospect of finding the acquisition price,
plus the money to carry out essential refurbishment work, as
well as a continuing revenue grant, seemed daunting. Nobody
was prepared to make such a commitment.

In 1976 it was announced that there would be a further
inquiry – on whether Sheffield Council should be forced to
buy the building from the owners. The company had served
a purchase order on the council claiming that the building
had no beneficial use.

What about a pub/cinema?

Empty buildings, however, almost invariably attract someone
who thinks they can put them to good use and the *Lyceum*
was no exception. Towards the end of 1977, the theatre was
bought for a sum 'believed to be in excess of £75,000', by
the Rentandin Property Company and a planning application
made to convert it into a public house, restaurant, cinemas
and discotheque.

The planning authority, Sheffield District Council, was
advised by its chief planner that there were no grounds for re-
fusal. The proposal would, in his opinion, preserve the building
and its plasterwork. The site itself was designated as cinema/
theatre and was in an educational, recreational and public buildings zone. Faced with the alternative of letting a listed building
deteriorate still further, planning permission was granted. Under
pressure from the various interest groups, it was made subject
to a number of conditions. These included:

- Plasterwork would be carefully restored and maintained;
- Structural alterations would be kept to a minimum;
- Dressing-room accommodation would be provided or preserved in the vicinity of the stage;
- The stage and fly-tower would be preserved;
- Means of escape incorporated into the scheme would be adequate for the total number of people likely to use the building if reinstated as a theatre.

Rentadin Property Company Ltd agreed to the conditions and drew up plans for the conversion of the building, but in April 1979 a local 'watchdog' for the trust spotted an agent's board outside the theatre. It appeared that parts of the building were to be sold or let off, one piece possibly for a furniture warehouse, though this was denied by the owners who had only applied for planning permission to incorporate four 'small retail outlets' into part of the street frontage of the building. The informant carried out his own research, posing as a furniture warehouseman. This particular 'scare' seemed to have been unfounded but his enquiries served to alert the trust to the fact that the plans, which accompanied the detailed planning application, appeared 'to contravene the terms of the agreement', blocking fire doors, making various new exits and entrances, creating a billiard hall on stage and possibly removing and relaying floors. It was also evident that the structure had not been maintained; the roof was leaking badly and part of the cornice had come crashing down.

As the building was listed, either the city council or the Department of the Environment could have issued a repairs notice but though visits were made no statutory action was taken.

By the end of 1979, it was apparent that the building owners no longer intended to proceed with the work for which planning permission had been obtained. Several of the shops had been let and the theatre, too, was made available at a rental of between £11,000 and £15,000 per annum. There were no takers. The trust considered whether some form of agreement could be reached whereby it was given a rent-free period in exchange for undertaking the necessary repair work.

In the meantime, another group of *Lyceum* supporters had got together to try to buy the theatre (which was by then expected to cost £150,000) and launched the 'Light the Lyceum' campaign in an attempt to raise the money. The trust and this new campaign joined forces.

Rock duo gets in first

While these organisations were working out the financial implications of renovating and operating the *Lyceum* as a theatre, the building caught the attention of other Sheffield entrepreneurs. In July 1981, *The Stage* reported, 'The Sheffield rock business has triumphed over local theatre enthusiasts in the race to buy the town's disused Lyceum. But the two music impresarios who clinched the deal in a surprise move last week have promised to give serious consideration to a proportion of theatre productions, once the venue is running at a profit.'

The new owners, Jo-Rockstar Ltd (a company formed by Kevin Johnson and George Webster, then operators of the city's *Limits* club), planned to make the *Lyceum* a regular port of call for big rock tours, converting the auditorium to accommodate an audience of around 2000, with a restaurant and nightclub to follow. They moved in and started the operation before any major work was carried out. In the preface to *Curtains !!!*, architect and theatre historian Christopher Bereton wrote 'facing reality, at least the present function will keep the building watertight and leave open the vague possibility that it might, at some future date, revert to theatre use – provided the acolytes of the pop groups don't tear off bits of the Rococo plasterwork in their enthusiasm'. It may have been of some small comfort to him to know that just two years later, Jo-Rockstar Ltd went into liquidation. The company said that the refusals of drink licences had made the project unviable.

In July 1982, the building changed hands once again. This time the owner was a company called Thermabbe Ltd which planned a mixed programme of rock music while promising the occasional opera and ballet tour. The proposal foundered when the true costs of refurbishment were revealed. The *Lyceum* was back in the hands of the receiver.

A way forward?

Once again the various interest groups, led by South Yorkshire Opera, came together to work out strategies for raising sufficient money to pay for the purchase, renovation, additions and revenue support. Despite the deteriorating fabric, each sale had increased the asking price.

It was at this point, that the suggestion was first made that the *Lyceum* might link up with the *Crucible*. Theatre Projects Consultants were commissioned by the *Crucible Theatre* to undertake a strategic study, paid for by a grant from the City of Sheffield. The report identified three options for the renovation of the theatre:

- it could be used cheaply and economically in a temporary fashion to provide much needed rehearsal and production facilities for both the *Crucible* and local amateur societies.

- It could be refurbished in a simple way keeping the existing structure backstage and front of house at a cost of approximately £1.85 million. There were two problems to this option; first whether the existing fly-tower was capable of resuscitation; secondly whether the existing stage would accommodate visits from major touring companies.
- It could be more comprehensively refurbished to provide facilities for the full range of professional drama, opera and dance (at an estimated cost of approximately £4 million).

The report also identified three management options for running the theatre:

- It could be city managed as well as city owned;
- The city could lease it to the existing or reconstructed board of the *Crucible Theatre* which would then manage the *Lyceum* in tandem with the *Crucible* and its studio;
- It could be run by a new non-profit trust which would lease the theatre from the city.

Outline operating budgets indicated that options one and three would incur operating deficits in the region of £200,000 per year while that option two would incur a deficit in the region of £150,000 (November 1983).

The trust offered to buy the theatre for £125,000 with the City and Metropolitan councils agreeing to put up some of the money.

An all singing, all dancing bid

Once again, another company was waiting in the wings, convinced that there was scope for a commercially profitable operation within the *Lyceum* building. Academy Enterprises (who had already taken over the *Palace Theatre* in Plymouth) put in a higher bid than the trust and in 1984 bought the *Lyceum*. The purchase agreement was made subject to their getting planning permission for considerable alterations to be made so that the building could be used as a theatre, restaurant and dance studio. The alterations were to include the installation of a flat floor in the stalls, 'stepping' the floor at the circle for restaurant tables, and erecting a new dance floor at mezzanine level in the wings.

Academy submitted plans in January 1985. Concerned at the deteriorating state of the building and keen to get in an operator who would see to the basic repairs, a special meeting of the city planning sub-committee was called to rush permission through in time for approval by the full council the following afternoon.

The meeting had to be postponed when Geoffrey Rowe, director of the *Crucible Theatre*, alerted council members to the statutory requirement to consult The Theatres Trust in London. *The Sheffield Telegraph* reported that the scheme could 'run aground on a little known Act of Parliament'.

The case was immediately taken up by the Victorian Society who opposed planning consent, on the grounds that the proposed alterations would be prohibitively expensive to reverse and jeopardise the possibility of the building reverting to its 'proper theatrical use'. The society made application for the *Lyceum*'s status as a listed building to be upgraded from II to II* – which, if granted, would increase its chances of receiving a grant from the Historic Buildings and Monuments Commission.

The Theatres Trust supported the case the Victorian Society had made and the Arts Council wrote confirming the importance of the building, 'We see the retention of the *Lyceum* building in a structural state which retains the basic theatre provision, as the only chance of providing a touring venue in the South Yorkshire area and for putting Sheffield on an equal basis with the other cities which are identified as strategic development areas'.

Though planning consent was granted (May 1985), it was made subject to a list of conditions relating to the preservation of the building's potential future as a theatre and to the renewal and refurbishment of the structure to bring it to a standard commensurate with its listed building status.

The cost of fulfilling the conditions effectively killed the Academy project and the theatre remained in the hands of the receiver.

Individual action

The campaign to save the *Lyceum* had been led by two key members of the South Yorkshire Opera – David Heugh, its chairman and Norman White, its producer. When the Academy bid failed, they took a courageous decision. Backed by the Royal Bank of Scotland and Sheffield City Council, they bought the *Lyceum* building for £101,000, using their own homes as security. To put their involvement on a firmer footing, a new trust was formed. While work was carried out to make the theatre weatherproof, the search for financial help was set in motion.

But by that time, local government was faced with the problem of rate capping and the dissolution of the Metropolitan Councils and Sheffield itself was embroiled in the ramifications of the miners' strike. Cuts were threatened across the board. Though supportive, saving the *Lyceum* was not one of the city council's top priorities. Even the most optimistic of the *Lyceum*'s supporters could not see a way forward. While the potential of the joint venture with the *Crucible* was seen as both 'exciting and enormous', the short-term view could not have been more bleak. The building was 'saved' but to what end?

The Universiade bid

Determined to push Sheffield out of the doldrums, the city council launched an ambitious project – hosting the 1991 Universiade, the World Student Games. To help secure the games, the city planned 'its largest ever arts festival'. This required a venue capable of receiving the major dance, drama and opera companies and attention turned once again to the *Lyceum*. Theatre architects, RHWL, were commissioned to carry out a design study for the refurbishment of theatre, working alongside officers from the city council and the staff of the *Crucible Theatre*. The study developed the idea of joining the theatres into a single operational structure. 'The proximity of the *Lyceum* to the *Crucible*, and the very differing styles of the two theatres, make a unique combination. The *Crucible* is a repertory theatre whilst the *Lyceum* will be suitable for touring productions. The *Crucible* has an open-thrust stage, the *Lyceum* a proscenium arch. The *Crucible* evolved in the theatre building boom of the 1960s and 1970s and the *Lyceum* in the late Victorian/Edwardian boom. The audience in the *Crucible* is all on one level, in the *Lyceum* they are stacked on three tiers. The character of the *Crucible* is modern; strong forms and bright colours whilst the *Lyceum* has highly sculptured surfaces and was subtly painted to highlight the decoration.' (Taken from the introduction to the RHWL study.)

The search for finance

The outlook was now a buoyant one. Sheffield City Council agreed to provide around £10 million for the Tudor Square project (which included work to other buildings – the *Crucible*, the Central Library and the Ruskin Gallery) and managed to secure a £4 million European Regional Development Fund grant.

It was also anticipating a 'generous' grant from English Heritage for what was by then a grade II★ building but English Heritage had just had its funding capacity reduced and had taken the decision not to take on any new commitments for the year. Frenzied political lobbying turned the situation in the *Lyceum*'s favour and a grant of £250,000 proved forthcoming. Significant additional sums came from the private sector (Hepworth plc donated £250,000 and Davy of Sheffield £100,000) and from a public appeal which raised £1 million.

Sprague's very fine auditorium is especially notable for its superb Rococo plasterwork which was meticulously restored in 1990. (*RL Photography*)

In postscript, Sheffield was to find that a Government ruling meant that the grant from the EEC resulted in an almost commensurate reduction in the council's overall capital expenditure limit. Sponsorship for the games fell below expectations and the city council, with support from the Sports Council, then had to fund a rescue package.

The refurbishment project

The theatre manager, Chris Reece, describes the 1990 *Lyceum* refurbishment in terms of an egg. 'We left the yolk (the auditorium), and the shell (the street façade) and dug away at the white (replacing the foyer, bars, circulation area and everything behind the proscenium arch).' The 'new build' element added about a third more space to the original building.

The main entrance was moved from the front corner with its domed tower to the long elevation fronting the main square (close to the entrance of the *Crucible*). Once a traffic artery, the square itself is now pedestrianised and paved over so the route from one theatre to another involves walking just a few steps across an open courtyard.

The new addition houses the main circulation route (staircase and lifts) and provides five levels of accommodation comprising three floors of dressing-rooms (108 spaces); a rehearsal room, green room and office space.

A completely new stage was added, served by a new 17m high fly-tower designed to house a full range of modern

lighting and technical equipment. With dimensions 12m x 12m, it is large enough to accommodate the productions of any of the major touring companies. Providing this facility involved demolishing the existing stage house and propping up the remaining structure until it could be supported by the new addition.

The auditorium was fully restored and the gilded plaster-work meticulously repainted in a predominantly gold and cream colour scheme appropriate to Sprague's original style. The newly built public spaces are contemporary in design, contrasting with and complementing Sprague's delicately detailed ornament.

The *Lyceum* finally reopened as a theatre on 10 December 1990. The project had cost £12 million.

Current operation

The first thing which had to be achieved was the drawing to-gether of the two separate and equally well-established groups (one having run the *Crucible* for twenty years while the other had fought a difficult campaign to secure the reopening of the *Lyceum*). Forging a new identity proved more difficult than had first been anticipated and the process is, to a certain extent, still a continuing one.

In terms of management, the *Crucible* staff took over the *Lyceum* and the joint operation is still serviced largely from the *Crucible*'s building where most of the administrative, technical and support staff are based. With its café/bars, restaurant and exhibition spaces, the *Crucible* complex is open to the public throughout the day. The box-office (extended when the *Lyceum* opened and now fully computerised) takes bookings not only for the three auditoria but also, on a reciprocal basis, for recreational (sports and leisure) venues throughout the city. The *Crucible* also houses the main catering operation and the food preparation areas (food is taken across to the *Lyceum* as required). If plans to mount 'in-house' productions at the *Lyceum* come to fruition, the sets and costumes will be prepared in the *Crucible*'s workshops.

The initial impression is that the *Crucible* is the workhorse supporting a very beautiful and rather refined partner. In fact, the *Lyceum* building is a strong income earner in its own right. As well as attracting good audiences, its elegant spaces are ideal for entertaining. For conferences, food is served in the *Lyceum*, enabling all three auditoria to be let without closing the *Crucible*'s public areas. The new additions to the *Lyceum* include an ex-

(*RHWL*)

cellent rehearsal space, marked out with the stage dimensions of both the *Crucible*'s main space and the *Lyceum*. This space is widely used by visiting companies as well as housing the Youth Theatre Company and hosting education activities and theatre workshops. The main hospitality areas and the business sponsors' club room are all housed in the *Lyceum* building, as is the development office.

The theatres currently (1998) receive revenue subsidies totalling about £1.3 million (a reduction on the peak funding of £1.5 million) from Sheffield City Council and Yorkshire and Humberside Arts. As the theatres share staff, support services and many overheads, it is not easy to work out exactly what pro-portion of the subsidy is required for the *Lyceum* but the chief executive estimates that, were it to be a separate entity operating purely as a receiving theatre, a subsidy of £400,000–£500,000 (more in line with the feasibility study estimates) would be sufficient. The 'lion's share' taken by the *Crucible* relates to its role as a producing theatre. The joint operation has a turnover of about £5.5 million a year.

The buildings now

The *Lyceum* has been exceptionally well maintained and shows little of the wear and tear which might be expected over seven years of constant use. This is achieved by setting aside a regular budget for maintenance and working to a planned five-year redecoration schedule.

The *Crucible* presents a more difficult problem as money is needed to renew rather than to maintain. It is now nearly thirty years old and needs to be updated in terms of its technical provision (there are no stage lifts) as well as some of the furnishings, fittings and decorations. Where renewals and redecoration work have already been carried out, the quality of the original design once again becomes evident. To its credit, the trust is seeking the advice of the original architects, RHWL, before making any more changes to the building. A lottery application is planned.

Further arts developments, including a new gallery, are planned for Tudor Square as part of Sheffield's 'Heart of the City' millennium project. Central to that concept is the *Lyceum Theatre* which, with its restored façade and its elegant new additions, provides the focal point of the 'Arts' square. The theatre is there as a result of the determination of a small group of people who appreciated its value – and incredible luck.

Other linked theatres

Partnership venues can be found in Manchester (where the Apollo Leisure Group links the *Palace* with the *Opera House*) and Bradford (where a single general manager is responsible for seven local authority run venues). A single management is also being developed to link the *Edinburgh Festival Theatre* with the *King's Theatre*. These theatres are all subjects of other case studies in this book.

Separately run but complementary venues can be found in Northampton (where the traditional proscenium arched *Theatre Royal* is situated adjacent to the multi-purpose *Derngate Centre*). The two venues are planning to submit a joint application for lottery funding.

The *Theatre Royal*, Plymouth has two differently sized and formatted auditoria within a single building, as has the *West Yorkshire Playhouse* in Leeds.

Sources of information

Lyceum, published by Sheffield Libraries to mark the reopening of the theatre

The newly built public spaces are contemporary in design. (*RHWL*)

When plans for the merger were first drawn up, it was envisaged that the *Crucible* would be the 'generator' promoting new writing and experimental work, with the *Lyceum* taking the more established touring product. What actually happened after the two theatres merged was that the *Crucible* tended to become more conservative to appeal to the audiences which were flocking to the newly opened *Lyceum*. The current chief executive for the theatres, Grahame Morris, aims to differentiate the spaces more effectively to make them truly complementary, using each for work most suited to its character rather than seeing one as the production company's repertory space and the other as the receiving house for touring product. Before joining 'Sheffield Theatres' he worked at the *Theatre Royal* in Plymouth, which has two differently sized and formatted auditoria within a single building.

Key Points

- Allowed to deteriorate for thirty years
- Identified in *Curtains !!!* as one of the finest of the 'Sleeping Beauties'
- Virtually written off when the *Crucible Theatre* was planned
- Achieved listed building status while threatened with demolition
- Three separate opportunities to purchase the theatre were lost
- Bought by two individuals on behalf of a preservation trust
- EEC-funded as an urban regeneration project
- Now run in partnership with the *Crucible Theatre*

Type of operation:
Receiving venue linked to the Crucible Theatre

Ownership and management:
Owned by The Lyceum Theatre Trust and leased to Sheffield Theatres Trust

Original architect:
1897 W G R Sprague

Architects for 1991 refurbishment:
RHWL

Listed:
Grade II*

Uses:

1897–1968	*theatre*
1968–90	*either closed or with intermittent use as a pop music venue*
1990 continuing	*theatre*

Current capacity:
1098

*'Above all, I want to ensure that the people of Edinburgh
see it as their theatre.'*

Councillor Lesley Hinds, Leader of Edinburgh District Council

Introduction

Edinburgh Festival Theatre is a celebration of theatre, its glazed façade proclaiming its presence within a street of solemn stone buildings. It is a place to see and be seen. As with many of the theatres featured in these studies, once reopened there is a sense of inevitability about the whole process. The refurbished *Festival Theatre* formerly *The Empire* suits its purpose so well that it is difficult to believe it could have been overlooked for so long. But for years the theatre stood empty, used only for bingo, while a whole range of other possibilities were being explored.

Once the decision was taken, the main partners demonstrated their commitment to the project and moved forward with commendable speed. Within three-and-a-half years, the theatre was purchased, the whole of the front of house and backstage areas were rebuilt, and the auditorium completely refurbished. It reopened in 1994. Edinburgh had got both its opera house and its Festival theatre, within a single space, and had created a new landmark for the city centre. It has also managed to retain what is considered to be one of theatre architects W & T R Milburn's finest auditoria.

Edinburgh's Opera House

Edinburgh's attempts to create an opera house date back to 1947 when the first international arts festival was held in the city, but forty years on *The Guardian* was reporting on the 'saga of the missing opera house', describing it as 'the longest-running tragical comedy farce' in the country (31 August 1990).

The first positive move came towards the end of the 1950s when Sir William Kininmouth was commissioned to draw up designs for a new 1400-seat theatre in Castle Terrace. This scheme got as far as the foundations being dug but then, for several years, remained just a 'designated' hole in the ground. Kininmouth was finally axed as architect for the project in 1972 when a revised brief was drawn up by the city architects. The estimated cost had risen from £4.5 million to £20 million but Edinburgh Corporation pressed on with the project. Despite some pressure to hold an architectural competition, RMJM, then led by Sir Robert Matthew, was awarded the commission. The scheme foundered when the Royal Fine Art Commission rejected the design. In 1984, after some abortive attempts to site the theatre elsewhere, RMJM's design was resurrected and, in a scaled-down form, secured the backing of the Conservative controlled council. But the political balance shifted and the project was shelved. In 1985, local surgeon Willie Souter took up the fight to raise cash for an opera house, setting up the Campaign for an International Opera Theatre in Scotland (CIOTS). This move was made in part to oppose a plan beginning to be promoted by the Apollo Leisure Group to adapt its Edinburgh theatre, the 3000-seat *Playhouse*, to receive the Festival productions. The COITS plan was for a newly built theatre to be sited in the port of Leith, two miles from Edinburgh's city centre. Feasibility studies were carried out but, as with its predecessors, the project came to nothing. The money which remained in the campaign coffers (about £1500) was eventually donated to the *Festival Theatre* the year after it opened.

While these 'new build' plans were being developed, other options were being explored. As early as 1975, architect James Dunbar-Nasmith (whose firm was subsequently commissioned to undertake the refurbishment of the building), identified the *Empire Theatre* as having great potential for opera and prepared a report for the Scottish Arts Council. By then, the building was being used as a bingo hall. Dunbar-Nasmith had to sign on as a club member before he was allowed into the auditorium.

Fifteen years on, Edinburgh District Council was persuaded of the viability of the *Empire Theatre* option and was on the verge of striking a deal when Mecca (who owned the building) was taken over by the Rank organisation. In the confusion which surrounded the take-over, the council failed to meet the cash deadline. Rank subsequently decided that it needed time to evaluate its property portfolio before making any decision. The theatre was finally bought by the council in 1991 for £2.6 million. The purchase of adjoining land and the shops which made up the street frontage of the theatre block, increased the price for the total site to £4 million.

The Theatres Trust's newsletter comments on the thirty-year search, 'Strange how a 1800-seat theatre on a principal thoroughfare could have been so frequently overlooked. How much cheaper these alterations and refurbishments would have been at any time over that period and how much time would have been saved in devising schemes for new opera houses.'

The second Empire

The *Empire Theatre* was the eighth theatre to be built on the Nicolson Street site since 1830 and the second to bear that name. The original *Empire Palace* was opened in 1892. Designed by Frank Matcham, it was the first of the Moss Empires chain. *The Scotsman* reported on its opening night, 'The theatre with its stately proportions and beautiful decorations stood revealed in all its grandeur and the audience, charmed with the brilliant spectacle, broke out in a loud and hearty cheer'. Unfortunately, this building was badly damaged in May 1911, when fire broke

The original frontage included retail units to the left and right of the theatre entrance (demolished in 1992).

out back stage. The illusionist Lafayette had accidentally ignited a stage drape. While the audience escaped unhurt (the safety curtain restricted the fire to the stage house), Lafayette and nine of his companions died in the fire.

Matcham came out of retirement to restore the damaged theatre. It was reopened in October 1911 but soon began to lose its appeal, as audiences, by then getting accustomed to the new cinema buildings, wanted more comfort. The Matcham theatre was replaced by the present *Empire Theatre* in 1928, one of the last to be designed by W and T R Milburn. James Dunbar-Nasmith writes, 'What it lost in originality, it gained in practicality for the Milburns produced one of the best auditoria in Britain for major lyric productions. In the succession of Empire theatres that they designed for the Moss organisation they steadily refined and adjusted the dimension of their auditoria until, with their Edinburgh theatre, they produced their most satisfactory; not so large as Liverpool or Southampton, but enabling every member of the audience to see the whole of the proscenium and to hear every note that is played or sung.'

From 1928 to 1963 the *Empire* was a variety, musical and opera house and, during the second half of this period, hosted many of the Edinburgh International Festival productions. In 1963, it closed for live performance and, like many others, was turned over to bingo. Mecca maintained the building for nearly thirty years despite the fact that towards the end of its tenure, the bingo club had only two hundred members.

From Empire to Festival

The newly named *Festival Theatre* opened on 18 June 1994 to a similar level of acclaim to that which had greeted its Matcham predecessor over a hundred years before. A press release explains the steps which had been taken to secure the theatre for Edinburgh.

A new spirit of partnership was emerging in the city; the importance of tourism to its economy had been recognised with Lothian Regional Council, Edinburgh District Council and the newly formed Lothian and Edinburgh Enterprise Ltd (LEEL), sharing a common goal of re-positioning Edinburgh as a major European tourist destination. LEEL and Edinburgh District Council commissioned John Myerscough to undertake an economic assessment. Further technical feasibility work was also commissioned.

The Myerscough work can now be regarded as a significant milestone. The report confirmed that the Empire represented the *best possible buy* with regard to the provision of an international lyric theatre and opera house for Scotland, and was fundamental in ensuring the future success of the international festival.

The report's concept of *affordable excellence* was the basis on which the case for acquisition was argued, winning all party support through both the district and regional councils. The Scottish Arts Council, Historic Scotland and the Scottish Tourist Board came on board and the show began in earnest.

By the end of 1991 an independent theatre trust had been established, chaired by the then Rt Hon. George Younger, MP, Chairman of the Royal Bank of Scotland plc and former Secretary of State for Scotland (now Viscount Younger of Leckie) and the design team, led by architects Law & Dunbar-Nasmith, had been formally commissioned. Organisations such as United Distillers, the Royal Bank of Scotland and the Dunard Fund committed themselves to supporting the trust, providing the first private sector pledges of a £4 million public appeal.

The concept of *affordable excellence* was evident in both the capital and revenue projections. In capital terms, the studies demonstrated that a first-class international operatic and theatrical venue could be created for less than a third of the cost of a comparable new facility. In revenue terms the Myerscough report suggested that a sustainable balanced programme (forty-six to forty-eight weeks based on high quality, large-scale works) could be achieved without subsidy by the third year of operation.

The refurbishment

While the Milburns had created an excellent auditorium, the commercial constraints imposed on them at the time had not allowed much money to be spent on the front of house. Designed to accommodate twice-nightly productions and geared to getting audiences in and out of the building as quickly as possible, the original entrance and foyer occupied only a small part of the Nicolson Street frontage with the rest of the area being given over to shops. Current theatre economics depend on audiences being encouraged to spend time in the bars, cafés and shops, exhibitions and hospitality suites. This 'open all hours' strategy stimulates community involvement; helps build audiences and produces revenue income. To create a front of house to service these needs, the buildings between the auditorium and the street were demolished and their sites incorporated into the new frontage.

The *Edinburgh Festival Theatre* now presents a visually stunning three-storey glazed façade complementing the historic stone buildings of collegiate Nicolson Street. From inside the foyer areas, people can look right along the street corridor to Robert Adams' Old Quad and get a view of his Register House, at the top of Princes Street, while the pedimented portico of Playfair's Surgeons Hall stands directly opposite the theatre. The concave curve of the theatre's frontage is angled and set back slightly from the building line with only its prow edging out to claim its presence in the street. During the day, the structure provides a break in the street pattern, its faceted glass reflecting its more austere neighbours. By night, the theatre shines out as a beacon of light and activity. The glazed façade is not just an architectural statement. It serves to open the building to the passer-by, to encourage scrutiny and to invite people in.

At street level, the new front addition houses the first of a series of café/bars. This one is designed to be seen as part of the street with no changes of level between the exterior and interior; the two being separated only by a simple glass screen. The effect is of a pavement café encouraging people to stop by. Once inside, they are immediately drawn into the theatre itself. A video wall shows extracts from the current production, the box-office opens up onto the single ground floor space, and the wide staircase (with adjacent lifts for those unable or unwilling to climb the steps) sweeps people up to other bars; exhibition areas; meeting and hospitality rooms; and on into the auditorium. Each of the three foyers feeds people into the auditorium at different levels (five in all) making the progress from the social area to the performance space a quick and easy one.

When announcing the debut season, Paul Iles, the theatre's first general manager, wrote, 'The first thing the Festival Theatre must be is *festive*. We must inspire that special social euphoria, the buzz of stimulated people interacting, common to the best theatres, wherever their whereabouts or whatever their programme.' The large, open foyer spaces, linked by a single grand stair and providing views from one to the other, help to make this theatre one of the most sociable and festive in Britain.

On entering the auditorium, the audience finds a subtly reworked version of the original space. The auditorium has been redecorated to a design, secured through a competition, which follows the style of the original rather than seeking to reinstate its colours, which were considered somewhat gloomy. ('We feel it is what the original architects would have done had a little more money been available at the time.') New ventilation, lighting and sound equipment has been fitted into the existing structure. For example, four panels of the dome were removed to accommodate lighting positions. When the stage was rebuilt it was given a flat surface to meet the needs of modern productions which meant that compensatory adjustments had to be made to the stalls rake (lifting it to the rear, and less noticeably, to the

sides) to retain the excellent sightlines of the original design. The 1928 seats were re-upholstered and refitted where they existed and copied where they were missing. Wheelchair positions were inserted with small ramps which could be raised to create level platforms.

Stage and backstage facilities were very restricted in the *Empire Theatre* but there was space to expand both at the sides of the auditorium and to the rear of the stage. The architects took full advantage of the opportunities this offered. The stage has been designed to accommodate a wide range of productions – from the largest available touring opera to a single performer – and to facilitate a practical and cost-effective backstage operation. It was hugely enlarged to 25m x 18m plus a rear scene dock, and a generous wing space on stage left – in total about 900m². At 25m high, it is now the largest stage area in Britain (though the *Royal Opera House*, *Sadlers Wells* and the *Lowry Centre* in Salford, may all claim precedence when their multi-million pound lottery backed projects are completed). An acoustic screen separates the main stage from the scene dock. When

closed it enables the dock to be used for assembling or storing the set of another production and when open it can be used to create a deep vista.

Dressing rooms for up to 120 performers and 110 musicians, all with natural light, are accommodated in a newly built four-storey addition. This building is of straightforward construction with the structural blockwork and services' ducting left exposed, allowing money to be concentrated on providing space and facilities.

The final bill for the refurbishment project came to £20 million (excluding the site acquisition costs). While the bulk of the money came from public funds, £4 million was raised through a public appeal with £1.25 million of this sum coming from the 'founders' circle' with 400 individuals and organisations each contributing £2,500.

The original budget had included a 'working capital' allowance of £600,000 to get the new operation off the ground. This became subsumed into the building budget as costs rose. Some of the money was spent on items which had not been included in the original calculations, e.g. a cooling system which would have involved redecorating the whole of the auditorium had it been left to a later date. The early 1990s were difficult years for the construction industry with companies securing work with unrealistically low bids and then becoming insolvent. At one point in the Edinburgh contract the stainless steel was removed and had to be repurchased. These problems led to delays. Contractors worked through the night to open on time. They managed it but at the cost of the money set aside to support the theatre programme.

The theatre in operation

Paul Iles recognised that it would not be possible to run the theatre without subsidy. To counterbalance the inevitable criticism, he aimed to make the theatre indispensable, bringing in as many people as possible so that they would form an attachment to the place. During the first year of its operation sixty-eight different productions were mounted, forty-eight of which were exclusive Scottish performances. Nine operas were shown with visits from the English Bach Festival Opera and British Youth Opera as well as Scottish Opera. Visiting dance companies included Scottish Ballet; English National Ballet; Birmingham Royal Ballet; the Siobhan Davies Dance Company; Rambert Dance Company and the Russian Army Ensemble. Concerts and drama productions were also hosted as well as light entertainment and ice shows. (Iles describes the *Festival Theatre* as having 'the best ice show stage in Britain after the *Blackpool Pleasure Beach*'.)

But the concept of the *Edinburgh Festival Theatre* had been 'sold' to the local authority and to the public on the basis of its being self-sufficient. When it became known that the theatre had run £300,000 over budget during each of its first two years of operation, the management was accused of incompetence. External accountants were brought in to appraise the operation. They reported that the theatre had been incompetently run but recommended, nevertheless, that regular subsidy would be required to support the programme in the future (confirming what many in the profession had already suspected to be the case). Edinburgh City Council then agreed to provide revenue support of £300,000 a year. By then, the pressure of the criticism levelled at the management during this period had led to the resignation of the general manager. Whether the Myerscough report's conclusions were strategically or merely inadvertently over-optimistic has to remain a matter for conjecture.

The policy of a mixed programme 'something for everybody' has continued with musicals, shows, comedy and children's productions interspersing a generous programme of dance and

The glazed facade serves to open the building to the passer-by. (*Edinburgh Festival Theatre*)

opera. With Edinburgh's *Usher Hall* currently (1998) closed until the money can be found for its refurbishment, the *Festival* theatre is also hosting more concerts. The theatre has productions throughout the year except for a two-week closure immediately following the Festival and odd days for set-ups and rehearsals by visiting companies. It now runs more or less within its budget, supported by the continuing £300,000 a year subsidy.

Economic analysis

Arts facilities are frequently cited as having a role as economic generators; putting more back into the economy than they take out in public funding. In this case, the claim was tested both through initial studies, when it was estimated that the project would create around 300 jobs Scotland-wide, and again once the theatre was operational. In 1994, after one full year, The City of Edinburgh District Council and Lothian and Edinburgh Enterprise Limited appointed economic consultants, Ekos Limited, to undertake a preliminary evaluation to assess the impact which the *Edinburgh Festival Theatre* had had on the city and regional economies.

The study looked at both the direct impact (i.e. employment opportunities within the theatre operation and money spent directly by the theatre and its employees) and at the off-site impact (i.e. expenditure on food, travel and accommodation incurred as a result of a day or evening out at the theatre). It took account of 'displacement' expenditure (i.e. the negative impact which the theatre had had on other leisure activities). The study did not, however, include any figures for money paid or spent by companies touring to the venue. The method of calculation used was one established in an earlier Scottish Tourism Multiples report.

The net additional annual income attributable to the *Edinburgh Festival Theatre* was calculated to be £1.35 million to the people in the Edinburgh and Lothian economy (or £1.54 million when Scotland as a whole was considered). The gross employment attributable to the theatre operation was assessed as being 288.9 full-time equivalent jobs in Edinburgh and Lothian and 339.7 FTEs for Scotland (excluding the employment generated during the construction period).

Other benefits include further public and private capital investment in the area in response to demand created by the theatre. This was assessed at £12 million. A more detailed study is due to be carried out to assess a longer period of the theatre's operation.

Theatres in competition

Though Edinburgh had long felt the need for a venue capable of housing Festival productions and large-scale touring productions from national and international opera and dance companies, the city did not lack theatres. Among the larger venues are the vast 3000-seat *Playhouse*, owned by the Apollo Leisure Group and used, predominantly, for the big long-run musicals; the *Royal Lyceum*, the home of the city's main repertory producing company; and the *King's*, owned and managed by the local authority as a touring house. Though a capital city, Edinburgh's potential theatre audience is not large. The population of Scotland as a whole is only just over five million (c.f. Bradford or Southampton each of which have larger populations within their catchment areas).

The *King's Theatre* had been struggling to maintain its position for some time. As the *Festival Theatre* became established, it began to lose both product and audiences. In April 1997, Graham Devlin was commissioned to work out a strategy for the two council-supported touring venues which would enable them to operate within the current levels of subsidy (i.e. eliminating the continuing deficits being incurred by the *King's Theatre*). He recommended that the theatres be run as a single operation by the Festival team with the *Festival* as the main lyric house. The *King's* would concentrate on drama with a more limited season (possibly about twenty-four weeks a year).

The merger was finally agreed on 20 July 1998 when the Festival City Theatre Trust was formed. If successful, the joint operation will avoid the reopening of one historic theatre leading to the total closure of another.

Sources of information

Press releases issued by *The Empire Theatre Project* and by *The Edinburgh Festival Theatre*
Building Study, *RIBA Journal*, May 1994
Building Design, September 1990

Key Points
- One of the finest lyric theatre auditoria in the country
- Well positioned on a city centre site with scope for further development
- Ignored during most of Edinburgh's forty-year search for a new opera house
- Auditorium refurbished within a newly-built enclosure housing the foyer, stage and backstage areas
- New glazed frontage opens the theatre to the city
- Now run as a joint operation with the *King's Theatre*

Type of operation:
Receiving venue
Ownership and management:
Owned by City of Edinburgh Council and leased to Festival City Theatres Trust
Original architects:
1928 W and T R Milburn
Architects for 1994 refurbishment:
Law & Dunbar-Nasmith
Listed:
Grade B
Uses:

1928–63	*theatre*
1963–91	*bingo*
1994 continuing	*theatre*

Current capacity:
1913

Theatre Royal, Glasgow

*'Scottish Opera is the outstanding success story in the
Arts in Scotland since the war and its greatest single achievement
is the acquisition and reopening of the Theatre Royal'*

1977/78 programme notes

Introduction

Many Victorian theatres come with the tag 'one of the prettiest auditoria in the country' but this one really is. Recently redecorated, the auditorium now glistens in an authentic re-creation of its original dark cherry, turquoise, cream and gold colour scheme. Those who would warn that 'all that glisters is not gold', would in this case be wrong. Historic Scotland encouraged the theatre to replace the meagre gold paint of the earlier restoration with a generous amount of gold leaf, highlighting the intricacy of the decorative plasterwork on the balcony fronts, proscenium and ceiling – 'a delicate combination of Renaissance strapwork and Rococo of excellent quality' (*Curtains !!!*).

Despite its Grade A listed status, the building was not always treated with respect. It owes its survival to the Scottish Opera Company which, in 1975, rescued it from its use as a television studio; raised the £3 million needed to restore the structure and convert it back to a working theatre; and then made it their home. The company has run the theatre and taken care of the building ever since. The *Theatre Royal* now houses not only the productions of Scottish Opera but a whole range of ballet, lyric work, world-class drama and children's theatre.

History

The *Theatre Royal* stands at the very top of Glasgow's Hope Street – the third theatre to occupy the site. The first was called *Bayliss's Coliseum and Opera House,* designed by architect George Bell and opened in 1867. Two years later Queen Victoria granted it a charter and it then became known as the *Theatre Royal.* While the name survived, the building did not. In 1879 it was totally destroyed by fire. A replacement was commissioned from theatre architect Charles John Phipps, opening in 1880 and be-

coming part of the Howard and Wyndham chain in 1888. But, at the beginning of 1895, this theatre suffered the same fate as the earlier building. Phipps was commissioned to reconstruct the building and his new theatre opened within the year, in September 1895. This time the *Theatre Royal* survived and, taking a quote from the theatre's own historical record, went on to 'enjoy a long and successful association with the best in the world of entertainment.' At least it did until 1956, when the owners sold it to the newly established Scottish Television – still to be associated with entertainment but in a very different way from previously.

The hiccup years

Scottish commercial television was in its infancy when it took over the Hope Street building. Journalist, Gordon Irving, writing in *The Stage* (November 1997), recalls the time he spent working in the theatre during what he describes as its 'hiccup years as a homespun television studio'. Office space had been created for him in one of the ornate boxes, partitioned off and lit by a small interior window. From there he could see the stage, used for filming productions ranging from TV soaps and westerns to the occasional performance by the 1960's stars, including, on one occasion, the Beatles. Many of the original stage hands had stayed on and learnt new skills. But the auditorium, itself, was radically changed to meet the requirements of a fledgling television studio. Seats were removed, the stalls were boarded over to provide a flat-floored working area, equipment was clamped to the plasterwork walls and various areas were partitioned off to provide for the company's ever increasing demand for office space. Scottish Television eventually recognised that it had outgrown the theatre building and moved into office and studio spaces which had been purpose-built on a site next door.

Scottish Opera moves in

The *Theatre Royal* had formerly been the leading lyric house in the city and was known to have excellent acoustics. When, in 1973, Scottish Opera discovered that it was to be vacated, it took immediate action. A campaign executive was formed under the direction of Gavin Boyd CBE which, with amazing speed, succeeded in raising £1.2 million from commerce and industry, £1 million from Government and £300,000 from private individuals. (These figures need to be translated into current values to appreciate the true extent of what was achieved – a multiple of five would give some indication.) With this money and generous bridging financial help from Glasgow District Council, Scottish Opera was able to buy the *Theatre Royal*; carry out a major refurbishment and undertake the work needed to reopen the building as a working theatre and opera house. Arup Associates were appointed as architects, with the team led by acoustics expert Derek Sugden.

The first performance was in October 1975. From a peripatetic touring company, Scottish Opera had graduated to become a company with its own base, enabling the artists and musicians to rehearse *in situ*, rather than, as previously, in a series of far-flung outposts scattered around Glasgow.

A showcase for the Opera

Scottish Opera is Scotland's only professional opera company, funded by, amongst others, the Scottish Arts Council to present productions in Glasgow and Edinburgh and tour throughout Scotland. In addition to the main touring role, the company has a number of other groups: *Scottish Opera Go Round* which takes opera to smaller venues; *Essential Scottish Opera* which presents piano accompanied highlights; and *Scottish Opera For All*, the company's community and education outreach unit.

The *Theatre Royal* provides Scottish Opera with a showcase and establishes its presence in the city from which it draws both audiences and funding. It is the visible tip of the iceberg, the small part of a much larger organisation which the public is actually able to see. The theatre launches most of Scottish Opera's main-scale tours and houses rehearsals once they get to the point where the company needs to rehearse *in situ*. Scottish Opera uses the theatre about twenty-seven weeks a year, mounting eight to nine opera productions (half of which are new and often premièred at this theatre). Scottish Ballet also spends about five weeks a year at the theatre (rehearsing or performing) and always opens its tours there. For the rest of the time, the theatre hosts visiting productions from the major touring companies including the Royal Shakespeare Company and the Royal National Theatre.

Though Glasgow and Edinburgh are within relatively easy travelling distance of one another and it might be thought that they each draw audiences from the other, with the two lyric theatres this does not appear to happen very frequently. Surveys conducted for the refurbished *Edinburgh Festival Theatre* show that only 1.3 per cent of its audience comes from Glasgow. Within Glasgow itself, the other main theatre is the 1800-seat *King's Theatre*, owned and managed by Glasgow City Council. Its larger capacity means that it takes in most of the big musical shows which come to the city.

The *Theatre Royal* is run by the management of Scottish Opera with only a small core team actually based at the theatre. The team comprises the theatre manager, the technical director, five technical staff, and the part-time and casual workers who look after the front-of-house and other services. The theatre (building and programme) is managed by Scottish Opera Theatre Royal Ltd, a subsidiary holding company set up by Scottish Opera when it acquired the building. This structure separates the theatre operation from the main opera company, ensuring that any losses incurred by the one do not undermine the future of the other.

Paying for the theatre operation

Neither Scottish Opera nor the Theatre Royal company receive any direct subsidy towards the day-to-day costs of running the theatre. They do, however, get grants to support the programming costs. Glasgow City Council gives regular grants, determined on an annual basis and varying according to the cost and quality of the productions. In 1997/98, the *Theatre Royal* received £80,000 from the city.

Until recently, the *Theatre Royal* received a grant of £120,000 from the Scottish Arts Council to support the cost of bringing in work from the national touring programme, but this grant has been withdrawn. Instead the theatre has to pitch with other Scottish companies for a share of the £100,000 available to help them extend their existing work.

Scottish Opera makes a regular contribution towards the cost of running the theatre. In 1996/97 it contributed £126,000 (representing 1.5 per cent of the opera company's total expenditure for that year of £8,621,000). In 1997/98, the amount needed was reduced to £40,000.

Faced with the increasing difficulty of buying-in good quality productions, the *Theatre Royal* management is looking to strengthen its links with other Scottish venues to promote joint tours from British and international companies.

Housing the company

While the theatre is seen as 'the home of Scottish opera', the bulk of the opera company's operation is actually housed elsewhere. The administrative team which handles planning, marketing, finance and fundraising for the company occupies a set of offices some distance away. The technical and production staff worked, until recently, in a number of spaces in different parts of the city. Concerned at the cost and impracticability of this scattered operation, reports were commissioned to look at the feasibility of building workshop and production spaces onto the back of the *Theatre Royal*. City-centre sites rarely prove to be the most cost effective way of providing large amounts of storage and workshop space, so it is no surprise that a less expensive and spatially more advantageous alternative was found. This involved building a purpose-designed industrial style 'shed' on a brown field site about ten minutes walk away. It provides space for building sets, processing scenery and costumes, orchestral re-hearsals, coaching rooms, and education work as well as an 'accessible' informal performance space.

The 'opera factory' cost £3.5 million and was funded by the Scottish Arts Council National Lottery Board (the first lottery application to be submitted), with matching funding provided by the Glasgow Development Agency and a commercial mortgage financed from the revenue savings on other rented spaces.

Scottish Opera and Scottish Ballet are two separate companies. While the basic structure remains unchanged (with independent boards, artistic direction, orchestras and performers), the two organisations have agreed to merge their service departments. In the longer term, a second 'opera factory' may be built to house what, by then, will be a single administrative and technical unit.

A continuing programme of improvements

Since the Scottish Opera first took over the *Theatre Royal*, successive front-of-house and backstage redevelopments have been carried out to make better provision for audiences and performers and to keep pace with technical developments.

The first of a series of major improvement projects was undertaken in 1990 when the public facilities were substantially extended. The architects for this work were MacLachlan and Monaghan. The front-of-house areas were enlarged to give more light and space, a new box-office was built and a café-bar (the Café Royal) was created. At the same time, the historic foyer, with its blond and rose sandstone floor, was redecorated, enhancing its ornate plasterwork. Facilities for corporate hospi-

With its delicate combination of Renaissance strapwork and Rococo and splendidly decorated circular ceiling the *Theatre Royal* is possibly the finest of C J Phipps' theatres to survive. (*Graeme Dixon*)

tality and private hire were also significantly improved ('entertain your clients with the perfect pitch'). Three new hospitality suites were provided (the Charter Room, the Boyd Room and the Gibson Room). This phase of the work cost £1 million with grants coming from Historic Scotland, the Glasgow Development Agency, the Foundation for Sport and the Arts, Scottish Brewers and many other public and private donors.

Planning for the next project began in 1994, with architects Law & Dunbar-Nasmith being commissioned to undertake a strategic study. Work started in 1997, concentrating, this time, on the redecoration and refurbishment of the auditorium. The stalls seating was replaced and reorganised to improve both comfort and the audience's view of the stage. The orchestra pit was extended and refurbished to provide enhanced acoustics and an improved environment for musicians (the existing pit went deep under the stage creating decibels of sound at levels which are no longer regarded as acceptable in health and safety terms). The small bars which are situated at different levels in the building were refurbished in the original style. This phase of the work was funded by the Scottish Arts Council National Lottery Fund.

Where furnishings and fittings had been lost or replaced, great efforts were made to trace the originals or to find their equivalents. In some cases the manufacturers were still operating and were able to find pattern books dating back to the late Victorian period. Restoring authenticity can create its own problems. Some patrons were upset to find a group of opalescent globes had replaced the 'beautiful crystal chandelier' which hung from the central dome – until it was explained that the chandelier had only been put there in the 1970s.

General accessibility around the building and specific provision for those with disabilities was also substantially improved. The stalls can now accommodate fourteen wheelchair spaces (made level by a series of individual lift-up ramps) and other seats have removable arms to enable the more mobile to transfer from their chairs to sit with companions.

From here on

The *Theatre Royal* has considerable strengths, not least of which are the quality of its building and the loyalty of its audiences. It has a very well-established group of subscribers, many of whom were drawn in during the campaign to buy the theatre and have attended performances on a regular basis ever since. The Scottish Opera link also helps attract support from the business community.

The aim is now to build on these strengths and the company is working to extend the appeal of its productions and draw in new audiences for both opera and ballet. But the closed frontage which the theatre currently presents to the street and the narrow entrances do little to encourage people to enter the building and may even deter people who are unfamiliar with the theatre from exploring what it has to offer. The current entrance was originally a side entrance, used to service the upper stalls and balcony levels, providing only secondary access for the stalls and dress circle. Future, longer-term plans include reinstating the original entrance round the corner in Cowcaddens Road and creating a foyer area to open up the building to its potential audience. It is not coincidental that the architects for the *Edinburgh Festival Theatre* (Law & Dunbar-Nasmith) were appointed for the most recent refurbishment work at the *Theatre Royal*.

With Glasgow's new *Concert Hall* now open just a few minutes walk away, the next major arts building project for the city could well be the extension of its *Theatre Royal*.

Key Points
- Grade A listed building
- Used as a TV studio from 1956 to 1973
- Bought by Scottish Opera and reopened as a theatre
- Used for Scottish Opera and Scottish Ballet productions and main rehearsals
- And as a touring house for lyric work, world-class drama and children's theatre

Type of operation:
Showcase for Scottish Opera and Scottish Ballet and a receiving venue
Ownership and management:
Owned and managed by Scottish Opera
Original architect:
1895 Charles John Phipps
Subsequent architects:
1973 Arup Associates
1990 MacLachlan and Monaghan
1997 Law & Dunbar-Nasmith
Listed:
Grade A
Uses:
1895–1956	*theatre*
1956–74	*TV studio*
1975 continuing	*theatre*

Current capacity:
1547

Georgian Theatre Royal, Richmond

*'Nowhere else in England is the earthy immediacy
of the 18th-century playhouse evoked so strongly'*

Iain Mackintosh writing in *Curtains !!!*

Introduction

The North Yorkshire market town of Richmond is full of
historic buildings jostling for space on its hilltop site. On the
corner of Friars Wynd, one of the narrow streets leading off the
main square, is what appears to be a simple stone barn. Tucked
between a couple of pubs, it was once a corn chandler's, then
a furniture repository and more recently an auction room. The
building served as a store of some sort for over a century, attracting very little attention until Edwin Bush, the history teacher
at Richmond Grammar School, began to investigate its background. Subsequent researchers established that the 'barn' was,
in fact, a theatre – the *Theatre Royal*, built in 1788. It is now
listed grade I and is regarded as one of the most important
buildings in the history of theatre in this country.

The 1982 edition of *Curtains !!!* describes the *Georgian
Theatre Royal* as a 'museum with occasional stage performances'
but many people in Richmond regard it as a working theatre
providing regular live entertainment for the town and its
surrounding area. While its age and historical importance
make this theatre unique, the problems which the managing
trust faces in seeking both to preserve a 'heritage' building for
the future and maintain it as a live performance venue, are
shared by many others.

This case study looks at how the building was restored
and given a new lease of life both as a working theatre and a
museum, reconciling the often conflicting demands of physical
authenticity and current operational requirements. The study
also demonstrates strategies for running a theatre within a
small town in a predominantly rural community.

Loss and rediscovery

The *Theatre Royal* was built by actor/manager Samuel Butler
as part of a circuit of five theatres, all within a fifty mile radius
of Richmond and all owned and operated by members of the
Butler family. Though Butler himself died in 1812, the family
continued to run the theatres until the 1830s. By then interest
was declining and, in 1842, after several years of occasional use,
the theatre closed. Solidly constructed and centrally located, the
space was soon put to other use. The pit was covered over and,
at some time in the late nineteenth century, a vaulted cellar was
inserted into the length of the building.

Moves to reclaim the theatre started in 1943, when the
building was acquired by the local council and theatre historians
Dr Richard Southern and Richard Leacroft were brought in to
advise on its restoration. After years of meticulous research, work
began in 1960 and three years later, the building was reopened

(The Georgian Theatre Trust)

as a theatre under lease to The Georgian Theatre Trust.

Eighty-five per cent of the original structure was eventually found to be intact. The cellar had, at first, seemed so integral to the building that people thought the performance must have taken place on the flat floor of the auditorium. Careful research revealed an earlier structure which meant that the intrusive vaults had to be removed before the authentic theatre could be restored. The original walls were found to contain clues to the earlier design with its sunk pit, raised stage, traps and machine-room, dressing-rooms and orchestra space.

The auditorium comprised a benched pit (stalls) area, eleven raised boxes (four at each side and three facing the stage) and courtyard style gallery. Sufficient of the interior structure had survived for the historians to work out how it had been decorated. There was evidence to show that the stage and auditorium had been lit by candles with open fires providing the only heating – one at the back of the stage and one in each of the two dressing-rooms.

Nothing of the exterior of the building suggested the use within. A single door opened direct from the street and from there a narrow stepped passage led, past the pay-box, into the auditorium. The gallery seats were reached by a tightly winding staircase.

The theatre today

One of the first things to strike the visitor is just how small this theatre is. The overall dimensions are only twenty-eight by sixty-one feet (auditorium and stage house). During its early years, the theatre claimed to have had a seating capacity of 450 but now less than half that number can be squeezed into its boxes and onto its benches. It is hardly surprising that the tightly packed audiences of Georgian times were accused of rowdiness and unseemly behaviour.

The initial building work aimed to re-create the original theatre, refurbishing what existed and restoring what had been lost. The bench style seating has been retained in the pit and gallery but, in the boxes, concessions have been made to the twentieth-century audience. Loose chairs (gilt, ballroom style) have been provided, inauthentic, but enabling those who occupy them to shuffle into the best position to see the stage.

The restored interior has been painted in a matched Georgian green contrasting with red *trompe l'oeil* curtains painted onto canvas at the back of the boxes.

Various work has been done over the years to make the building operable and provide basic facilities. For the 1963 re-opening, a small foyer was created from a store-room and three garages (adjacent to the theatre and owned by the nearby Turf hotel) were leased and converted to provide a bar and café as well as a link route through to the backstage areas. A double-door entrance had already been created from the Victoria Road frontage to provide access to the 'cellar' when the original theatre was being used as a store. This became the main entrance for the theatre. In 1969, the building was further extended to provide a scene dock, technical workshop and additional dressing-rooms and to improve the get-in. Since then, the initial heating system has been improved and the 1963 stage replaced.

The museum

In 1979 a small museum was built to help explain the theatre to its many visitors and to house valuable archive material. It occupied the upper floor of two former warehouses at the back of the theatre. Subsequent work enabled space to be found at ground-floor level and in 1996 the museum was moved and substantially redesigned. It now has four galleries and a small shop.

The museum tells the *Theatre Royal*'s history through original documents, engravings and photographs and explains the development of theatre design from the ancient Greek period onwards. The display includes the oldest complete set of Georgian scenery in Britain (a woodland scene painted in 1836); a unique collection of playbills from 1792 to the 1840s; as well as costumes from that period. Wall paintings depict the Georgian audience; a re-made groove system demonstrates how the scene changes were achieved; a 'thunder run' hangs from the ceiling (with a rope to pull to make it work) and the sounds and bustle which would have been heard in the original theatre (re-created in recordings) echo like happy ghosts through-out the galleries.

Live performance

However imaginative the techniques used to re-create an atmosphere, the essence of any theatre lies in the interaction between the performers and their audience. The closeness of the one to the other, the tightness of the overall space; and the sense of immediacy which this creates are integral to the experience of being in a Georgian theatre. Those who rediscovered this building wanted to bring the space to life, not only as a physical reconstruction but as a working playhouse.

But the form belongs to another era when the audience was squeezed in tight; seat prices were high (the old playbills show that in the early days a visit to the theatre was expensive –

(*Clive Barda*)

seat was sold, the income raised would rarely be sufficient to pay for the product. The solution was to open the theatre on a regular but limited basis, raising money to subsidise the costs and only mounting the number of productions which could be supported in this way. A whole range of work was shown – from jazz to classical music and from light comedies to full drama.

The programme continues to be a varied one with the theatre now mounting between sixty and ninety productions a year, showing both professional touring product and amateur work. Recent events include music (The Konevets Choral Quartet from St Petersburg; subscription concerts; Kenny Ball and His Jazz Men; The Dalesmen Folk Group and Northumbrian Pipes); opera (Richmond Operatic Society; visiting singers and small touring groups); drama (including *The Tempest*, *Pygmalion*, *The Importance of Being Ernest*, Ayckbourn's *A Chorus of Disapproval* and Tennessee Williams *The Glass Menagerie*); music hall, poetry and comedy. The theatre also runs a youth theatre for the ten-to-sixteen age group with thirty members meeting once a week and mounting one production a year. How do they manage to do it?

The theatre operation

Richmond's *Georgian Theatre Royal* and museum is kept going by its many supporters. The organisation has only two full-time professional staff – the theatre manager, Bill Sellars (TV producer best known for the Yorkshire based series *All Creatures Great and Small*), and his assistant Carol Wilkinson – both of whom give far more time than the amount specified in their 'job descriptions' and work for salaries far less than their skills justify. Only two other people receive any remuneration for their work – one is responsible for the technical side of productions and the other helps with the accounts. Both are part-time. They are supported by a team of over 120 volunteers who staff the box-office, bar and shop; provide front-of-house, backstage and technical services; and act as guides throughout the long summer season. Little money is available for marketing so the theatre relies on mailing its 'regulars' list of 1500 and promoting its productions through the town's tourist and hotel network and the Georgian group. Most productions are limited to one or two nights, with companies visiting other venues in the region (e.g. Darlington Arts Centre) being persuaded to add on an extra day to play in Richmond. The theatre is closed completely during January and February with March showing amateur productions only.

Responsibilities are divided between two separate companies: The Georgian Theatre (Richmond) Trust Limited and The Georgian Theatre Productions Limited (both registered

three shillings for a box seat, two shillings for the benched pit and one shilling for the gallery); and family style groups of players toured the circuits. A full house would then have provided sufficient income to pay the company, run the building and make a good profit.

Current licensing allows the *Theatre Royal* to seat 229 but considerations of comfort and sightlines reduce this figure to less than 200. Auditoria with comparable seating capacities are now found mostly in arts centres and community halls and tend to be flexible 'performances spaces' rather than proscenium arched theatres. The touring companies of today serve this market, offering a very different style and range of product from that for which the *Theatre Royal* was designed.

The trust could have decided to put on the occasional period style production to demonstrate the historic theatre to a select audience. Instead, it set out to provide a varied programme which would cater for the needs of the people living in Richmond and its surrounding area today. It soon became apparent that nearly every production would cost, rather than earn, money. The logistics of the space meant that, even if every

charities). The former runs the building and museum side while the latter runs the programme. This structure serves a number of purposes. It separates the trading arm from the charitable activities (maximising the tax benefits) and helps to protect the core organisation from the financial risks involved in mounting productions.

The theatre building is still owned by Richmond Town Council and is leased to The Georgian Theatre (Richmond) Trust Limited at a peppercorn rent. The museum building is owned by the trust while the front-of-house buildings belong to Bass Breweries (which owns the adjacent pub) and are let to the trust on a long lease.

Georgian Theatre Productions Limited receives approximately £20,000 a year in revenue support, split between the county, district and town councils and Yorkshire and Humberside Arts Board. The rest of its operating budget comes from income earned from ticket sales, from donations, and a small amount from investments. In the year ended March 1997, the company earned about fifty per cent of its £65,000 operating budget. Ticket prices now range from £3 to £10 for most performances with the 'best seats' going up to £15 on special occasions.

The cost of running the building and of the museum are the responsibility of the trust which operates to a separate budget. In 1997 it raised about £17,500 from admission charges, theatre hires, catering and sales, towards its operating costs of £36,000. The rest of the money came from donations, grants and gifts. The salaries of the staff are split between the trust and the productions company.

The theatre is fortunate in several respects. Prestigious performers and groups are prepared to visit Richmond for the experience of working in what has been described as a 'truly magical space' and to spend the extra time required to adapt their work to its special conditions. The building's unique history ensures strong local support and its grade I listed status helps the trust secure funding for restoration and improvement work. The theatre also has an established tradition of royal patronage.

On the other hand, the trust has to face the joint problems of running a theatre in a rural area and of maintaining an historic building. The surrounding area is not a rich one and there are few businesses from which sponsorship can be sought. As with other small arts organisations, work has had to be undertaken as and when funding could be raised. Throughout its development, grants from local authorities, funding bodies, and trusts have been supplemented by generous amounts of voluntary work and by individual donations.

The trust raised £162,000 for the work it carried out between 1994 and 1996, including a grant of £50,000 from the Heritage Lottery Fund. This was part (phases one and two) of a programme of improvements and concentrated on the museum and related areas.

The ACE Lottery application

Used to operating on the 'step by step' principle, the trust turned next to the Arts Council of England (ACE) lottery fund to help it realise phase three of its planned capital programme. This phase will seek to improve front-of-house facilities, upgrade equipment and redecorate some of the interior of the theatre. The initial intention was to apply for £100,000 (the cut-off point for small projects) raising a further £65,000 through grants and appeals.

ACE responded with a grant of £30,000 and a requirement that the trust commission a detailed feasibility study. Architects Allen Todd, who had advised the trust on earlier work, were appointed to undertake the study and began by organising a seminar to bring together the various interest groups – design professionals, theatre management and consultants, and local authority conservation and museum officers – to discuss the issues before any design work was undertaken.

There was unanimous agreement that an accurate analytical survey should be undertaken as part of the development phase, including an investigation of the fabric, with 'as found' plans and sections and drawings showing the evolution of the theatre from 1788 to the present day. 'It is the one thing we would have liked to inherit from the earlier work and it is what we should hand on to our successors.' (John Earl, consultant to and former Director of The Theatres Trust.)

Once again, consideration of the options available highlighted the problems inherent in preserving the historic authenticity of a unique grade l listed building while maintaining a fully operational working theatre to provide live entertainment for its local audience.

A full restoration would entail reinstating the fore-stage to its original dimensions (now believed to have been cut back between 1820 and 1835 to create the orchestra pit); searching for evidence to justify installing traps and other equipment in the stage; lighting the theatre to re-create the 1788 candle quality and improving the decor to make it look more authentic, and reinstating original bench style seating in the boxes. The effect of all this, if implemented, would be to reduce the seating capacity, lower the ticket prices in the boxes, make the stage less suitable for dance and reduce the well used under-stage dressing-room space by filling some of it with equipment.

On the other hand, Arts Council accessibility requirements for a space this size would involve making provision for five or six wheelchair spaces, widening entrances, removing steps and tight corners, and providing good lighting and colour contrast in the decorative scheme to help the partially sighted. If implemented, these would effectively destroy the authenticity of the building.

A middle way had to be found. A possible solution was worked out but it required more space than was available within the existing theatre complex. The trust negotiated with the brewery which owned the adjacent public house and succeeded in obtaining its agreement to lease the theatre a strip of land (1.5m wide) along the forecourt. This additional land would enable the front of house to be extended to increase bar/foyer space and provide sufficient space for a lift to be installed. The lift would provide access to the rear of the gallery where wheelchair spaces could be made available without impinging on any of the original structure at ground-floor level. The lift would also link the front-of-house areas and provide access to a new bar/café created, at gallery level, above the existing front-of-house addition.

It is now clear that the cost of this final phase is likely to be nearer £700,000 than the £165,000 envisaged when the lottery application was first submitted. The trust is hoping that the work undertaken in phases one and two will be accepted as providing the core of the partnership funding package. The application was still being prepared when this book went to press.

If the grant is forthcoming and the proposed work is put in hand, the trust is confident that it will do much to secure the future of the theatre both as an historic building and as a place of live entertainment.

Source material

The Georgian Theatre, Richmond, Yorkshire: Rediscovery of the Theatre, a paper by Richard Southern
Richmond Preserv'd, a paper by Percy Corry
The Georgian Theatre Royal and Theatre Museum Official Guide

Key Points

- An historic theatre of unique importance
- Determined to be more than a museum
- Runs a regular but limited programme of professional and amateur productions across the art forms
- Operates to a minimal budget supported by a network of voluntary workers
- A 'brainstorming' session held as part of the feasibility stage of lottery application to resolve potential issues of conflict between museum, heritage, theatre history, production and operational interests

Type of organisation:
Receiving venue for small-scale work and theatre museum
Ownership and management:
Owned by Richmond Town Council and leased to The Georgian Theatre (Richmond) Trust Limited
Original architect:
Unknown (built 1788)
Reconstructed under the supervision of:
Dr Richard Southern and Richard Leacroft (reopened 1963)
Current architects:
Allen Todd
Listed:
Grade I
Uses:

1788–1842	*theatre*
1842–1943	*storehouse*
1943–63	*museum*
1963 continuing	*theatre and museum*

Current capacity:
229

Palace Theatre and Opera House, Manchester

'One of the bravest gambles in the history of theatre outside London'

Michael Kennedy writing in *The Daily Telegraph* in 1981

Introduction

Two theatres, very similar in size and style, lie about half a mile apart in the centre of the city of Manchester. They are the *Palace Theatre* and the *Opera House*. Rivals for many years, their fortunes rose, fell and rose again together. During the 1980s, they came under joint ownership and have continued to be run as complementary venues within a single organisation since that date.

Their history follows that of many of the big variety houses of the period. Built to catch the profitable late Victorian/ Edwardian boom years, the middle of this century found them struggling and threatened with closure. They were 'saved' by an entrepreneurial local team. A charitable trust was set up which, led by one man's generosity, bought and refurbished the *Palace* and then moved on to reopen the *Opera House*, establishing the two theatres on the touring circuit and continuing to run them for several years. The early 1990s saw another change when the theatres were bought by the Apollo Leisure Group, an expanding theatre management company with interests throughout the country.

These two theatres were both built by commercial enterprise; pulled out of decline and re-established through local initiative; and then reclaimed by the commercial sector to meet another end of the century boom in variety – this time in the form of the large-scale musical tour.

Early years

In 1889, a London business consortium offered shares in a new company floated to build a 'Palace of Varieties' in the centre of Manchester, drawing audiences from the five million people then living within a thirty-mile radius of the city centre. The *Palace Theatre* was opened two years later, packed to its 3675 capacity.

(The theatre now has 1996 seats.) Toying unsuccessfully with ballet in its first years, the theatre went on to concentrate on what attracted the audiences – variety – and did so successfully for many years before moving on to full length musical shows and reviews during the 1920s and 1930s. It continued to adjust to market demands, hosting the popular performers of the 1950s and the 'beat shows' of the 1960s. By this time the theatre had become part of the entertainment group, Moss Empires (bought in 1959).

In 1912, the *Palace* acquired a rival, a neoclassical structure in nearby Quay Street, first called the *New Theatre* and then the *New Queen's Theatre*. It had some difficulty in establishing itself within the Manchester theatre network but that changed when, in 1916, Sir Thomas Beecham brought his opera company to the theatre. For the next fifteen years or so, opera played a significant role in the theatre's programme with visits by the Carl Rosa Company, British National Opera Company, and D'Oyly Carte. In recognition of the success which Beecham had bought the theatre, it was renamed the *Opera House* (1920). In the early 1930s, it was bought by one of the other large entertainment companies, the Howard and Wyndham chain, and from then on concentrated on big name drama productions and on musicals rather than opera.

Boom turns to bust

While both theatres continued to promote live shows, each began to find it increasingly difficult to attract audiences. In 1967, the *Palace* experienced its 'worst year ever' and press reports began to appear of talks between the two management groups – Moss Empires and Howard and Wyndham – to determine which of the two theatres would close. Rumours of impending closure continued for more than a decade.

Demonstrations were mounted and petitions put to Manchester City Council urging them to buy the *Opera House* to secure the future of live theatre in the city but these efforts came to nothing. By 1977, it was evident that if either theatre was to survive it would need financial assistance from the local authority and that such support would only be available for one. According to a report which appeared in *The Guardian* (February 1978), the Howard and Wyndham management team, having failed to sell the *Opera House* to the Greater Manchester Council (GMC), precipitated a crisis by threatening to close its remaining theatres in Manchester, Liverpool, Birmingham, Bristol and Oxford – a move which would have destroyed the Arts Council's touring circuit. Subsequent talks resulted in the Arts Council and GMC providing a guarantee against loss to secure the autumn 1977 season.

At the same time, Moss Empires announced that 'with regret, due to the extreme shortage of commercial attractions the *Palace Theatre* will close at the end of November'. Pressure increased when it was revealed that a 'group of Arab oil sheikhs' was seeking to buy and demolish the *Opera House*, to use its site for a luxury hotel. The *Manchester Evening News* commented 'this paper has already said that the time for positive action is overdue. The arrival of the Arabs underlines that.' (November 1977)

The 'rescue' bid

Faced with the closure of both major touring venues, the GMC agreed to allot £150,000 towards the purchase of one of the theatres and a further £15,000 per year to subsidise its revenue (November 1977).

Initially, local interest focused on the *Opera House* because of its 'cultural traditions' but two years previously, the Arts Council had commissioned theatre consultant John Wyckham to look at the potential offered by each of the two theatres. He concluded that the *Palace* could be brought up to a standard to take all but the very largest operatic productions without major structural change and that the work could be completed within a twelve month period for around £600,000. The cost of achieving a comparable standard of provision at the *Opera House* was estimated to be around £2.5 million. After months of argument about which theatre to support, the GMC voted thirteen to two in favour of the *Palace*.

At this point, Raymond Slater, director of the Manchester based property and engineering company Norwest Holst, took over the leading role. Described by the press as 'Yorkshire-born self-made millionaire (or thereabouts) with a passion for the arts', he had already launched a campaign to raise the money to buy

the *Opera House*. When Howard and Wyndham did not respond to his initial bid, he turned his attention to the *Palace* and proceeded to buy the freehold from Moss Empires for £150,000 (payable in six annual instalments). The theatre changed hands in May 1978.

A charitable trust was set up with unpaid directors drawn from representatives of commerce, industry, the arts, civic life and the two local authorities, GMC and Manchester City Council (MCC). Raymond Slater gave the theatre to this trust. A decision then had to be made as to the scope of the refurbishment needed. Michael Kennedy, a trustee at the time, wrote, 'The trust had two choices: to "do up" the theatre almost as it was before, with inadequate pit and dressing-rooms and backstage facilities, for less than £1 million or to try to raise the £3 million for a complete facelift and for a stage enlargement which would enable the biggest opera and ballet productions to be mounted without the reductions and omissions which for years had left provincial audiences to complain justifiably that they only saw second eleven London shows.' (*The Daily Telegraph* 17 March 1981)

The trust decided to go for the more ambitious project. Its members were encouraged throughout the decision making process by the interest shown by the management of the *Royal Opera House* (ROH) in establishing a non-London base for their company. The trust thought that Manchester was being identified as a second home for the ROH, similar to that of the Royal Shakespeare Company in Newcastle. Had this not been the case, it is arguable that the trust would not have opted for what was to prove a very expensive scheme, that of extending the whole of the stage and backstage of the *Palace*. The choice might even have stayed with the *Opera House*.

The Arts Council promised a contribution of £400,000 from its by then somewhat stressed Housing the Arts Fund while the local authorities' financial commitment remained at the levels allotted to the original proposal (GMC £150,000 and MCC £350,000). Raymond Slater led a public appeal and approached private enterprise to raise the rest of the money. Robert Scott, who had overseen the building of the *Royal Exchange Theatre* and successfully managed that venue, was bought onto the team as managing director of the Palace Trust. Now, Sir Robert Scott, he went on to front Manchester's Olympic bids and is currently chairman of the Greenwich Millennium Commission.

The Palace Theatre refurbishment

In order to extend the stage area, the trust had to acquire a small part of an adjacent office building then owned by Standard Life

Palace Theatre interior. (*Apollo Leisure*)

prevailing taste. However, the truth it seems is that Manchester Palace of Varieties Ltd received a War Damage Repair Payment in the late 1940s to reinstate the exterior but did not spend it. Eventually the War Damage Commission told the company to either use the payment for its given purpose or return it. The theatre was then re-clad to meet the deadline.

Insurance Company who argued that a 'piecemeal' sale would undermine the value of the rest of the property. Not a man to be put off once he had decided on a course of action, Raymond Slater decided to buy the whole of the 2¼-acre block in which the theatre was situated at a cost of £2.25 million. Robert Scott explained how it happened, 'This was an amazing piece of bravura support by Slater. We needed twenty foot, but were told if you want the building you must buy all five which make up the estate. It sounded like buying the British Empire – Bridge-water House, Dominion House, Africa House, Asia House, India House.'

This purchase enabled the theatre to build its stage and backstage extension. A section of the office block was retained to house some of the theatre accommodation, the rest was to be let as commercial office space. This purchase was seen, in part, as an investment which would provide a regular income base to support the theatre operation.

As well as refurbishing the auditorium, work was carried out to improve facilities both for the audiences and for the visiting companies. In the front-of-house areas, direct access was opened up to the adjoining Palace pub providing patrons with a new bar and restaurant complex, and the foyer and existing facilities were extended and improved to include cloakrooms, a bookstall and a lift to the old gallery – renamed the Grand Tier. Backstage

The *Curtains !!!* entry in respect of the *Palace Theatre* reveals that, 'Darbyshire's splendidly opulent facade was obliterated by unprepossessing faience tiles in 1953', without offering any explanation for the change. It had been assumed that the flat 'contemporary' yellow tiling scheme was a misguided but considered attempt to modernise the building to meet

improvements included digging out a pit capable of taking the largest orchestra of 110 players; extending the stage depth by twenty feet and raising its height by twelve feet to accommodate the Royal Opera Company's stage sets; new lighting and sound systems and dressing-room facilities for 150 artists. The *Palace* was also the first theatre in Europe to install the Box Office Computer System (BOCS). The architects for the work were the Manchester practice of Smith & Way with Clare Ferraby designing the theatre's red, gold and brown interiors. Over £3 million was spent, with the stage alterations alone costing £750,000. The burden of funding the bulk of this work lay squarely on Raymond Slater's shoulders.

Building on success

The *Palace Theatre* reopened in March 1981. Its first year of operation proved to be both a financial and artistic success. The planned break-even budget was turned into a six figure profit with the theatre mounting some twenty weeks of opera and ballet as well as the most sought after touring shows available at the time.

The traditional concept of marking down ticket prices when national companies visit the regional theatres was successfully challenged, with the *Palace* raising the prices of its best seats to levels comparable with those charged by London theatres. By 1984, companies were queuing to book into the 2000-seat theatre where they could regularly expect to play to near-capacity audiences.

Meanwhile, the former rival, the *Opera House*, had been bought by Mecca and was being used for bingo. With a string of 'sold out' productions at the *Palace* to its credit, the trust decided to buy the *Opera House* and reopen it as 'the home of the major West End musicals in the North West'. It achieved this objective in 1984, paying Mecca £320,000 for the freehold and spending in excess of £500,000 on refurbishing the theatre. Both theatres continued to be run by the Manchester Palace Theatre Trust Ltd. With the two theatres, the trust was able to mount extended runs of successful musicals at the *Opera House*, while the *Palace* took in the visiting ballet, opera and drama companies. This policy challenged existing preconceptions that theatres outside London could not support more than a few weeks of any single production. Breaking down this prejudice was not easy. 'We had to fight and fight to get producers to consider anything other than a six week run for the *Palace Theatre*. The big revolution was in 1985/86 when we got *Evita* into the *Opera House* on an unlimited run basis, the first time ever outside London.' (Robert Scott)

Neither venue drew on public subsidy other than that given by the Arts Council to the national companies to enable them to tour. Both houses made profits on the theatre operation and Manchester was firmly established on the arts map. The gamble had paid off with dividends.

The Royal Opera House, though it sent some touring product to the specially extended and refurbished *Palace Theatre*, never pursued its interest in establishing a second base.

All change again

The one problem which the trust had been unable to solve was the funding gap on the loans Raymond Slater had arranged to complete the refurbishment of the *Palace*. While the operational picture at both theatres was rosy, the income was never sufficient to make any significant inroads into the capital debts, all of which were being carried either by Raymond Slater personally or by his company Norwest Holst. Neither was in a position merely to write them off and the trust certainly could not meet them even though some finance had been raised through the Palace 100 Club.

The only solution was for the trust to hand over the theatres to Raymond Slater for the significant consideration of taking over the debts. The Charity Commissioners were consulted and they agreed to the arrangement on condition that the position be advertised so that other potential buyers, perhaps prepared to pay more than Mr Slater, could put in bids. Not surprisingly, no-one did, since at this time the debts were running into several million pounds. A new company, Manchester Theatres Limited, was created to replace the charitable trust and the original trustees became members of an advisory council.

By the end of the 1980s, the recession was beginning to hit both the construction industry and the property market. Raymond Slater, whose boldness and generosity had so benefited Manchester audiences and the Arts in the region, loosened his links with the theatres before leaving Manchester altogether to live in Guernsey. Manchester Theatres Limited was successively bought by March Holdings and then by a company called Vista, a group with broadcasting, restaurant and night club interests. By the end of 1990, Vista, itself, was experiencing problems and needed to recoup its investment capital. In January 1991 the theatres were sold on to Apollo Leisure in a package deal valued at around £7 million.

Throughout the six years in which the two theatres were run in tandem, first by the trust and then by Manchester Theatres Limited under various owners, the management team remained in place and the public saw no operational change. When Apollo took over they put in their own team and Robert Scott became an Apollo consultant.

The Apollo operation

The Apollo Leisure Group is one of the UK's largest private entertainment companies, with theatre, hotel, bingo and social club and licensed operations through the country. It currently owns or manages twenty-five theatres and concert halls, four of them in the Manchester area.

Initially the *Palace* and *Opera House* were run as a single entity from the *Palace Theatre* but in 1996 a small team was appointed to oversee the *Opera House* to give each theatre a separate identity. The main administration remains at the *Palace* servicing both venues and technical and support staff are moved from one to the other as needs arise. The theatres currently employ about forty full-time staff between them with a further 160 or so on a part-time or occasional basis.

The bulk of the theatre operation is undertaken centrally. All bookings are arranged at Apollo's Oxford headquarters. The group also mounts some productions in association with Barry Clayman Concerts which tour its venues. Each venue is run to be financially viable with profits (and any losses) accruing to the company. The main profits tend to be made during the longer runs of the most popular productions. *Les Miserables*, for example, filled the *Palace Theatre* for over eighteen months and recently returned to play to 98.8 per cent capacity audiences for a further two-and-a-half months. During a separate eighteen month period, the *Opera House* hosted *Phantom of the Opera*. The profits from runs such as these feed back into the system, supporting low earning periods and producing funds to buy new theatres and improve the existing buildings. The ability to schedule tours to a string of large theatres throughout the country obviously gives Apollo considerable negotiating power.

Both houses run a mixed programme of touring product taking the major opera and ballet companies as well as drama and dance. When one has a long run, the other takes the shorter tours. The third Apollo owned venue in Manchester city centre,

The Opera House. (top, Paul Tomlin / bottom, Apollo Leisure)

the 3500 (seating and standing) Labbatts Apollo, takes most of the popular music events.

The *Palace Theatre* has a maintenance team of three full-time staff with a further two staff being based at the *Opera House*. They undertake all the day-to-day maintenance of the two buildings retouching the decorations 'continuously' and repainting to a regular schedule. When major works are required, they are authorised and financed centrally. In 1997, the stalls in the *Palace Theatre* were reseated and the whole area was recarpeted. Work on the dress circle is scheduled for next year. At the *Opera House*, Apollo renovated the main façade and have also made technical and backstage improvements. A problem which remains to be tackled is that of accessibility. Originally refurbished before provision for those with disabilities became mandatory for Arts Council funded building projects, the two theatres are ill-equipped in this respect.

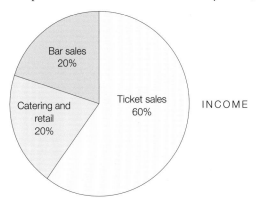

INCOME

Ticket sales 60%

Bar sales 20%

Catering and retail 20%

An all-win solution?

With theatres having to pitch in the open market for disappearing product and battle for an adequate share of local authority funding to ensure their day to day survival, the Apollo alternative must seem an attractive one. The centralised management system certainly has its advantages. When the purchase of the two Manchester theatres was announced, Sam Shrouder, Apollo operations director, stated, 'They are two of the most important theatres in the country. The very best shows that tour go to one of these two theatres.' Each of these theatres now receives some forty-two to forty-four weeks of good quality live entertainment a year at no cost to public funds. They are efficiently run and maintained by experienced theatre managers. They are unburdened of capital dept and supported by a commercially viable organisation.

Being part of the Apollo network should also strengthen the theatres' position when they are faced with competition from the lottery backed *Lowry Centre*, currently being built just a few miles away in Salford. The complex is to include a 1650-seat auditorium and is already seeking to attract the large scale touring companies for its opening season. It will be bidding its exciting new building and wide-ranging facilities against the Manchester theatres' larger seating capacities; established position in the touring network; and, most significantly, Apollo's superior negotiating power.

Despite the advantages, there is something missing from the Manchester operation. The most obvious lack is that of daytime activity. The doors open shortly before the performance starts and close soon after the curtain falls. The *Palace*'s restaurant is gone, even the box-office is closed for much of the time (tickets are booked through Apollo's centralised booking service). In this the theatres are no different from those in London's West End on which their operational style is based but do contrast with most of the other venues in these studies.

Perhaps more significantly, what appears to have been lost in the change from charitable trust to commercial company is the vitality which comes from a continuing involvement with the local community and from an individual personality shaping the programme in response to what he or she perceives the audience responses to be. There is no local board of trustees, no business club, no Friends to support the less popular productions and, though school tours are promoted, there are no educational activities encouraging experimentation or building an audience for the future. It is perhaps indicative of the central promotions approach that the audiences for drama (even award winning drama) and for children's work are so disappointingly low (ten per cent capacity for some children's productions). To draw

people in for productions other than the musicals and the occasional major opera and ballet tour may well require a more hands-on management style.

The management has recently taken steps to try to change this situation. An audience development officer was appointed towards the end of 1997 whose first task was to concentrate on improving contacts with the local schools.

Postscript

This was, in parts, a difficult case study to piece together and was only completed with the help of Sir Robert Scott who corrected some of the 'misinformation' gleaned from press cuttings and filled in the gaps. Commenting on the story of the two theatres, he observed that it served to demonstrate 'the cyclical nature of theatre – possibly if Moss Empires or Howard and Wyndham had known about the success of Andrew Lloyd Webber musicals they would never have sold.'

Source material

Apollo Leisure Palace Theatre and Opera House Information Pack

Key Points

- Two lyric theatres each threatened with closure
- Survival plan drawn up for one
- Involves massive site purchase and major refurbishment, with much of the cost financed by a local businessman
- The success of the first theatre, enables the second to be reopened
- The capital debt forces the sale of both properties
- Now owned and managed by a commercial company

PALACE THEATRE

Type of operation:
Receiving venue for large-scale touring productions
Ownership and management:
The Apollo Leisure Group
Original architects:
1891 Alfred Derbyshire & F B Smith
Auditorium reconstructed:
1913 Bertie Crewe
Architects for 1979/80 refurbishment:
Smith and Way
Listed:
Grade II
Uses:
1891–1978   *theatre*
1979–81   *closed for refurbishment*
1981 continuing *theatre*
Current capacity:
1996

OPERA HOUSE

Type of operation:
Receiving venue for large-scale touring productions
Ownership and management:
The Apollo Leisure Group
Original architects:
1912 Farquharson, Richardson & Gill
Architects for 1984 renovations:
Smith & Way
Listed:
Grade II
Uses:
1912–79   *theatre*
1979–84   *bingo*
1984 continuing *theatre*
Current capacity:
1929

Chipping Norton Theatre

'The house has all the characteristics of a traditional theatre which might once have been found in any town at any time in the last 150 years, but is now extremely uncommon'

The Theatres Trust

Introduction

How did a traditional Georgian style theatre come to be built and survive in the small Oxfordshire town of Chipping Norton? The answer is that, despite initial appearances, it did not happen quite this way. The building is old but it was not originally designed as a theatre. It was built as a citadel by the Salvation Army in 1888 to provide an alternative to the Victorian music halls and all the temptations which they offered. Though not a theatre, is was a place of live entertainment with a seated audience and a small proscenium style stage where the bands played – in many ways a perfect small auditorium.

With an ideal building ready and waiting, rich and influential supporters, and an enthusiastic local community eager to lend a hand, this could be seen as a 'silver spoon' project. But a small country town (population then 4000) is an unlikely place in which to establish a professional theatre. That the theatre was not only established there but developed into a significant resource for the whole region has to be credited to the skill and determination of one woman, Tamara Malcolm, who founded the theatre and then remained as its director for over twenty years.

Creating the theatre

The Salvation Army gave up their citadel in 1962. When Tamara Malcolm and her family first moved to Chipping Norton in 1968, the building was used as a store and auction room for second-hand furniture but, as actors, she and her husband immediately appreciated its potential as a theatre. In 1973, a 'for sale' notice appeared on the door and within days Tamara had persuaded a 'very rich friend' to guarantee the £6500 purchase price needed to secure the building. John Malcolm, who had helped set up the *Traverse Theatre* in Edinburgh knew some of the pitfalls involved. He ensured that one of the first people to look at the building was the local authority's fire officer. The second was the local bank manager.

Fundraising started in earnest with a 'buy a brick' campaign and cake stalls while the surrounding area was scoured for potential supporters. A trust was formed and the new theatre company moved into the citadel, using it to build the sets for their first production in the town hall. A wide range of local people was drawn into helping turn the building into a theatre. At this stage everybody worked for free, including the electrician and the plumber.

The building was in good structural condition (built of stone within a terrace) but needed to be cleared and cleaned before work could start on the conversion. The auditorium already existed with benches in the 'stalls' and surrounding gallery space very similar to that of a Georgian theatre (c.f. Richmond *Theatre Royal* on page 54). It also had the beginnings of proscenium and stage where the Salvation Army bands had played but the stage area itself had to be created, dug out of the hill on which the building stood. Initially, the citadel housed the whole operation – the auditorium, the stage, toilets tucked into the back of the gallery space, and the box office doubling as the only management space.

The Malcolms drew on their network of friends and contacts within the business to get the theatre programme going. Their established relationship with the *Theatre Royal*, Stratford East led its actors, writers and directors to travel regularly to the Chipping Norton theatre to work on productions. From the day the theatre opened, everybody who worked there was paid – the actors, the projectionist, the front-of-house staff and the cleaners. The support money came from fundraising, including a 5p a week lottery and street collections. Both the town council and the district council made small revenue grants (approximately £300 and £700 a year, respectively). Tamara Malcolm was the only full-time member of staff.

Raising the capital

Chipping Norton lies in the middle of an area where much of the UK's wealth and influence is concentrated. This was to prove a distinct advantage. Legal advice was provided by Lord Goodman who drew up the Articles of Association and early in the fundraising campaign, the trust was introduced to a potential donor who, when approached, offered an interest free loan for the full purchase price provided that he remained anonymous. Ten years later, the loan was converted to a donation.

The Arts Council's Housing the Arts fund and the Gulbenkian Foundation both contributed towards the cost of the conversion work and enabled the theatre to buy the next door cottage and its garden. These spaces were converted to provide front-of-house facilities, administrative offices, dressing-rooms and a stage workshop.

Many of the fittings used in the original conversion came from other buildings – the lights from an early cinema, the carved mahogany bar from a local grocery shop where it had long served as a cheese counter.

The theatre opened in August 1975 and has continued to grow both as an organisation and in physical terms ever since that date. It presents a comprehensive and eclectic programme of professional theatre, classical music, folk, jazz and cinema serving a large rural area and attracting audiences in excess of 30,000 a year from Cheltenham to Oxford, and from Banbury to Witney and beyond. It also has an art gallery, a popular exhibition space. As well as showing productions by visiting companies such as the Moving Theatre Company, SNAP and Union Dance, performances by local groups and by visiting individual artists, *Chipping Norton Theatre* has a successful youth theatre and organises classes and workshops for both adults and children. Every summer, holiday workshops led by professional actors visit surrounding villages.

Building on success

Over the first decade or so, *Chipping Norton Theatre* concentrated on developing its activities – widening the range and number of its performances and building up its youth theatre and education work.

By 1991, it was apparent that the organisation was beginning to outgrow its existing premises. A phased programme of additions and improvements was drawn up and an appeal was launched to buy an adjoining property. The following year work began on an adjacent building in Goddard's Lane, a small town house which had been extended to include a converted cooperage. This provided a much-needed annex, with dressing rooms, a rehearsal room, backstage facilities, administrative offices and a new computerised box office and shop. (Phase one of the planned capital programme.) The new building opened in April 1993. The theatre raised the £262,000 needed in two years with major donations from the Foundation for Sport and the Arts, West Oxfordshire District Council, The Gatsby Foundation and Oxfordshire County Council. The completion of this project released sufficient space in the original building to make it possible for the theatre to consider moving on to the next phase.

With a donation of £20,000 from Cherwell District Council already in hand, an appeal was launched for the £544,000 required to pay for phase two. The work in this phase was designed to improve audience facilities, including provision for the disabled patrons; add another twenty-three seats in the auditorium (about half of which could be removed to create a pit area); and convert spaces formerly occupied by offices and dressing-rooms to provide more spacious foyer, bar, box-office and front-of-house areas. Structural alterations were to be made to the whole of the stage including the construction of a tower providing two metres' clearance over the proscenium arch to allow scenery to be 'flown' (enabling the theatre to take a wider range of touring product), and a new cinema screen with electronic masking was to be installed to improve the quality of the cinema presentation. Additional land needed to be purchased so that the stage could be 'squared off' and its depth increased from 4.42m to 9.14m. Technical equipment was also to be improved and the heating, lighting and services upgraded to meet new and higher standards. The plan was to complete this phase of the work by August 1996 so that the newly refurbished theatre would reopen in time to celebrate its twenty-first birthday.

First in line for lottery funds

It could be seen as merely fortuitous that *Chipping Norton Theatre* had a fully worked out capital programme waiting to be funded just when the National Lottery was announced but carefully planned 'opportunism' is a vital part of any theatre operation. Writing in the magazine *Prompt* (February 1997), Tamara Malcolm observes 'It is my experience that small organisations with little "career clout" have always to be in the vanguard as applicants to new funding systems if they are to have any chance of success. At first the politics that initiate new money are still fresh in the minds of those whose task it is to supervise distribution. All too soon the pressures of the increased numbers of applicants and the bigger institutions will cloud over the original

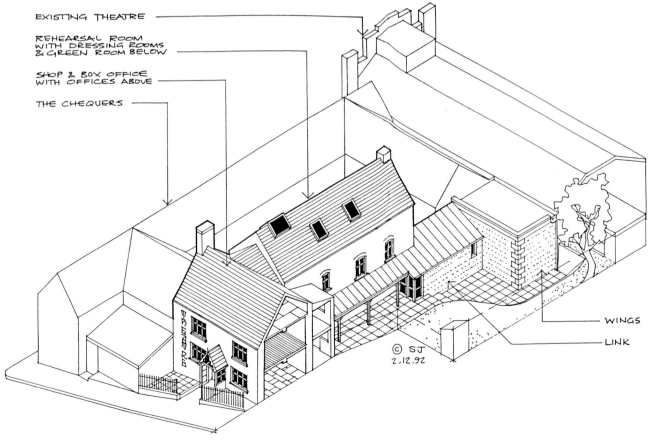

EXISTING THEATRE

REHEARSAL ROOM
WITH DRESSING ROOMS
& GREEN ROOM BELOW

SHOP & BOX OFFICE
WITH OFFICES ABOVE

THE CHEQUERS

© SJ
2.12.92

WINGS

LINK

raison d'être.' The theatre was determined to be in that very first batch of applicants and submitted the documentation on 4 January 1995, the day the floodgates opened. Its reference number was 004.

The new system worked to the theatre's advantage with the QS assessor recommending that the building contingency allowance be increased by 400 per cent. In the event, *Chipping Norton Theatre* was awarded a grant of £678,520, with the work it had already completed (phase one) providing the bulk of the partnership funding.

The theatre reopened in October 1996 with a 'sparkling' auditorium, a new stage – double its former size – and new front-of-house areas. The Arts Council's lottery criteria require that artists and craftspeople are involved in all funded projects, so inspired by the Palladian Theatre at Sabbioneta in Italy, where the audience is painted on gallery walls, and the contemporary *trompe-l'oeil* paintings at Ragley Hall, Tamara Malcolm invited the Ragley artist Graham Rust to work at Chipping Norton. The aim was 'to create an atmosphere of fun in the foyer and bar, so that the audience would then receive the performance with an open and generous mind'. Pantomime characters now cluster in groups around the bar and foyer areas in a light-hearted tribute to *commedia dell'arte.*

Current operation

Chipping Norton Theatre runs a year round programme of live performance and film, six days a week plus matinées. It still mounts its own pantomime and has an active youth theatre but the bulk of its performances are single night or short runs by touring companies – including new and experimental work. Last year there were sixty-six performances of the pantomime which filled the theatre to ninety-four per cent of its capacity. As the only cinema in the area, it screens a selection of films, mostly those on current release but including a programme of world cinema. The theatre also mounts a series of exhibitions featuring, in the main, the work of artists practising in or linked with the region. While the theatre itself is closed during July and August, workshops are held in the villages and the programme of films continues.

Five staff now work full-time at the theatre (four administrative and one technical stage manager) together with three part-time box-office staff, a projectionist, a front-of-house supervisor and two cleaners. The whole operation runs to an annual budget of nearly £250,000, excluding the cost of buying-in productions. The programme creates a surplus of about £90,000, with the bulk of the running costs being met from grants, sponsorship, fundraising, hires, and trading. (The shop, for example, is leased to the Oxfordshire Craft Consortium.)

Grants come from Southern Arts (£17,510 towards the live programme), West Oxfordshire District Council (£22,500), Cherwell District Council (£3700), Chipping Norton Town Council (£750), Parish Councils (£800), The Foundation for Sports and the Arts (£10,000 development grant for a three-year period only). All these figures relate to the year 97/98.

Each performance is priced according to its cost, with tickets for professional music, dance and drama ranging between £7.50 and £14.50 (with concessions). Films sell at £4.00 with matinées at £2.50.

Tamara Malcolm with the artist and his murals.
(*Jason Lowe © House and Garden/The Condé Nast Publications Ltd*)

The future?

The improvements are complete, the work has been paid for, the programme is fuller than ever, the activities are more varied and, despite the intentions of the original builders, the occasional music hall draws the audience in.

Success of this kind does not come easily. *Chipping Norton Theatre* has had to fight hard to retain the revenue subsidies on which its future depends and has managed its resources with both imagination and skill.

There are some who would say that running a full-time professional theatre in a rural community is just not feasible. Tamara Malcolm and her colleagues have demonstrated just what can be done. The objective now is to enjoy the new facilities and use them to further strengthen the operation.

Key Points

- 200-seat theatre created from a Salvation Army citadel
- Situated in a small town serving a rural community
- Offers a full and varied programme including film
- A fully professional organisation with paid staff

Type of operation:
Receiving house for small-scale touring companies, with cinema and 'in-house' pantomime production
Ownership and management:
Owned and managed by Chipping Norton Theatre
Original architects:
Built in 1888 (architects unknown)
Architects for conversion and refurbishment:
Agremead Architects
Listed:
The building is not listed
Uses:

1888–1962	*Salvation Army citadel*
1962–84	*auction room and store*
1984 continuing	*theatre*

Current capacity:
233

'Commerce, which wealth and elegance supplies,
here bids at length a Theatre arise'

From the prologue to the opening performance in 1782

Introduction

The *Grand* is not a flamboyant theatre. It is a simple stone building standing quietly a few yards away from Lancaster's busy town centre. The original builders slotted it into an existing row of tightly packed cottages, its façade forming part of a continuing street frontage. The theatre is now more isolated, marooned in an area of semi-wasteland, cleared many years ago for a redevelopment scheme which never materialised. But like the *Windmill* in Soho, the *Grand Theatre*, Lancaster can proudly boast 'We never closed'. The theatre building has been kept going as a place of entertainment, in some form or other, for 216 years.

Its history mirrors that of theatre buildings throughout the country – except that the *Lancaster Grand* survived where most of the others did not. It has been a theatre; a concert hall, museum and lecture room; and a cinema as well as an occasional bingo hall. At one point, the prolific theatre architect Frank Matcham had a hand in its design. Early this century, the building was partially destroyed by fire. Forty years later, a compulsory purchase order was issued for its demolition. It is now owned and managed by the Lancaster Footlights Club as its own home and as a venue for other amateur productions.

Though one of the oldest theatres in the country, the *Grand Theatre* Lancaster has rarely, if ever, hit the headlines. Georgian in origin, only the modified shell of the original building remains so it is not regarded as a heritage building of comparable significance to the *Georgian Theatre Royal* in Richmond, Yorkshire (see page 54). It has not had the benefit of large amounts of public money being invested in its future nor been the subject of any major refurbishment scheme. The theatre has been kept open and given a new role through the dedicated efforts of a small amateur group, raising what money they could to run a programme and to make step-by-step improvements to the building.

At the beginning of this century, almost every town had a theatre. It might have been expected that many of them would have been taken over by the thriving network of amateur dramatic and operatic societies and run by the enthusiastic volunteers who keep these societies going. In fact, the situation at the *Lancaster Grand* is a rare one.

This case study demonstrates both the difficulties facing a small amateur organisation and the considerable achievement of the Lancaster Footlights Club in keeping a programme going against the odds and maintaining a valuable resource for the local community.

(Ian Grundy)

Beginnings

The original theatre opened in June 1782 under the ownership of Messrs Austin and Whitlock, who ran a circuit of theatres at Chester, Manchester, Sheffield, Newcastle upon Tyne, and Whitehaven. No plans exist of it in its original state, but playbills remain advertising it as having a pit, lower boxes, upper boxes and gallery. For many years, it was known simply as 'The Theatre' but acquired the title 'Royal' in 1803, not by charter, but after a single visit from the then Duke of Gloucester.

During the 1830s, theatres throughout the country were losing favour with the upper and middle class audiences who were looking for recreation of a more 'uplifting' or genteel nature. The *Theatre Royal* closed at the end of the 1841 season but the building was immediately bought by a local architect, Edmund Sharpe, who converted it to house concerts, lectures and a museum, setting up the Lancaster Athenaeum Co. Ltd. These uses proved popular enough to justify extending the premises – in 1856 a neighbouring plot was purchased to accommodate an enlarged stage or concert platform.

The building changed hands again in 1884 when it returned to its original theatre role and was renamed *The Athenaeum Theatre*. Frank Matcham was brought in to redesign the stage extension and add a fly-tower but all this was lost in 1908 when fire broke out and gutted the building. The replacement interior, designed by architect Albert Winstanley (also responsible for the *Lyceum* at Crewe), was constructed within the walls of the Georgian original. The whole process took seven months enabling the theatre to reopen in the same year. The name was changed again, possibly to reflect its more lavish interior, and it became the *Grand Theatre*. Despite the name, the *Grand* was still a relatively small theatre. At this point in its history it had a seating capacity of 900.

By the 1930s, with the quality of its programme declining and its audience dwindling away, the theatre was put up for auction. It was purchased by a local entertainment chain who added a projection room and ran a mixed programme of cine-variety, films, straight plays and performances by local amateur societies. The operation was bought out by Union Cinemas and then by Associated British Cinemas (ABC), both of which ran it as a film only venue. ABC reintroduced repertory in 1947 but then put the theatre up for sale, placing a covenant on the deeds of purchase which stopped the building being used to show films. (ABC owned two other cinemas in the town.)

Home for the Lancaster Footlights Club

The building owes its survival to the Lancaster Footlights Club, an organisation which, though not as old as the theatre, has its own history. Its origins lie in an organisation called the British Drama League which was founded in 1919 to support readings and productions of contemporary works, neglected by the commercial theatre of the time. The league rapidly became the focus for amateur theatre, with affiliated groups being set up throughout the country. The Lancaster Footlights Club was formed as part of the league in May 1920.

The club first hired the *Grand* for a production in 1922 and continued to present plays there until 1935. After the 'film only' years, the amateurs were once again given access to the building with the Footlights productions returning to the *Grand* in 1947.

The decision by ABC cinemas to sell the cinema brought about a period of frantic activity, with four major local amateur societies, the Footlights, LADOS, Red Rose and the Vale of Lune, forming a joint committee to discuss the possibility of purchasing the building. ABC pressed for an early decision as there were other offers to be considered (including possible conversion to a garage). Lancaster Footlights Club decided to take the initiative and, acting on its own, agreed to purchase the theatre (including two cottages, a yard, and some adjoining land) for £7000. When it proved difficult to raise a mortgage within the limited time available, part of the purchase price was lent by individuals from the club and the other societies. A non-profit distributing company was set up to present repertory at the *Grand*.

Several attempts were made to bring professional product into the theatre. From 1951 to 1955 a newly formed company, the Castle Players, based themselves at the *Grand*. The players mounted over 200 productions during that period but the arrangement was not without problems. The professional company claimed that the amateur productions destroyed continuity and lost them audiences and asked for 'compensatory' payments to be made by the amateur groups. The company, though 'professional' could barely make enough money to pay its young actors (both Pat Phoenix and Frank Findlay appeared in productions) and folded after four years.

A bid was made to set up another company in 1956 and secure Arts Council funding but this came to nothing. That company folded in February 1957.

Let's knock it down

The club's nine years of hard work looked like being wiped out when, in August 1959, the city council served a compulsory purchase order (CPO) on the theatre building. The surrounding cottages were regarded as slum housing; the area was designated for industrial development; and the theatre was in the way. Footlights briefed Counsel and argued for the preservation of the theatre. The case was helped by the Ministry of Housing and Local Government placing the building on the supplementary list of buildings of architectural or historic interest (September 1959). The resulting public inquiry excluded the theatre building (and the properties within its ownership) from the CPO along with two historic warehouses. The remaining buildings were demolished but the proposed development plan was never implemented. The site now stands asphalted but empty – retained for potential road improvements. The theatre is now listed grade II (1975).

During the mid-1960s, discussions were held with the city council regarding the possibility of extending and improving the *Grand* to house a long-planned civic theatre. The money initially offered was insufficient to enable the Footlights to find a replacement building and the council then discovered that it would be unable to get rid of the film embargo which ABC had placed on the building 'in perpetuity'. The council subsequently modified its proposals and converted a redundant chapel to provide a performance/cinema space – the *Dukes Playhouse* which opened in 1971. The opportunity to secure a role for the *Grand* which would attract regular revenue funding was lost.

The theatre has continued to be run by Lancaster Footlights Club and let to other amateur companies, since that date.

Refurbishing the building

The history of the building is evident from its exterior. Windows were inserted into the plain Georgian façade when it was converted to museum use and two additional structures can be seen, one at either end of the original building. They house the Victorian fly-tower and the 1930's projection room.

Since Footlights took over the building it has had to work hard to maintain and improve the structure and facilities. When the club first moved in, supporters clambered up ladders to paint the decorative stucco work. During the early years, the stalls seating was reorganised to improve comfort and access (the theatre now seats 465); a theatre bar was opened, the act drop curtain replaced; and the wall to the side of the stage renewed when a dangerous structure notice was about to be issued. In

(*Ian Grundy*)

the 1960s, improvements were made to the heating system, the backstage areas were reorganised and the front façade repainted.

Much of the work was done by teams of volunteers, led by club members with building expertise. The current Footlights president, Ray Langley (a qualified civil engineer) and his brother-in-law, a master builder, have looked after the building since the club first moved in. Much of the equipment needed had to be got on the basis of 'beg, borrow, steal or con'. From 1958 to 1966 additional income was raised when the theatre was let on a regular basis for bingo sessions organised by local football and cricket clubs. This was put into the building fund.

New emergency electric lighting had to be installed in 1978 to replace the gas lights and that same year, the theatre bar was remodelled. Grants of £2000 from the city lottery and £1000 from the local brewers helped pay for the work.

By the late 1970s, it was becoming increasingly evident that several larger-scale repairs had to be carried out. The project was by then well past the 'brush and bucket' stage. The roofs of the adjoining cottages needed to be renewed; the stage switchboard was wearing out; the safety curtain needed attention and the interior needed to be decorated. Footlights drew up a phased programme and set about finding the money. With the help of a professional fundraiser they set up the first of a series of covenant schemes to raise about £75,000 over a period of six years. The following two schemes were launched to raise £95,000 and then £134,000. Now on the third scheme, the money has been used to maintain the fabric, refurbish the auditorium and improve backstage and front-of-house facilities. The entrance to the theatre is directly off the street, past a small box-office and straight into a foyer. This area has been enlarged and a coffee bar added in space created by resiting the old toilets. The existing staircase to the stalls was also resited to provide more space in the foyer.

For the last forty-seven years, Footlights has carried the responsibility for refurbishing and maintaining the 200-year-old historic theatre. Since setting up the covenant scheme, the club has been investing upwards of £10,000 a year in its building. During the whole of its occupancy, the largest single donation which Footlights has ever been given is £30,000 – awarded by the Foundation for Sport and the Arts two years ago to pay for the installation of a toilet and related provision for disabled people.

The Footlights operation

Lancaster Footlights has approximately 300 members about fifty of whom regularly participate in running the building and the organisation. The theatre and club are managed by a general committee and a number of support groups (covering membership, building management, bar and catering, marketing and front-of-house activities) as well as a covenant secretary and a lettings officer (both voluntary posts).

The club now mounts seven productions a year including one for its junior members and the annual pantomime. The 1997/98 season showed productions of *Relatively Speaking* (Alan Ayckbourn); *The Madness of George III* (Alan Bennett); *Cinderella*; *When We Are Married* (J B Priestley); *The Dresser* (Ronald Harwood); *Separate Tables* (Terence Rattigan) and *Big Friendly Giant* (Roald Dahl). Each production runs for five evenings (with two preview evenings for members) while the pantomime has a slightly longer run which includes two matinée performances. Club members make most of the sets, costumes and props. Footlights also operates a costume hire business and, to a lesser extent, loans out sets and equipment having acquired the stock of a local theatre set hire company which went into liquidation.

The theatre is hired (on a fixed-rent system) by many other groups in the area including five musical groups. There are also occasional visits from professional touring groups who have discovered the building (organised on a share of take or straight hire system). At 465 seats, the theatre is quite large for the amateur drama productions (averaging thirty to forty per cent capacity audiences) but suits the operatic groups and the pantomime very well.

The bars are open for productions and 'club nights' and the theatre runs a morning coffee bar every Saturday for both members and the general public. The box office is staffed throughout the week from 10 a.m. to 3 p.m.

The whole operation is run by four part-time staff which includes two cleaners.

Sources of income

The club receives one hundred per cent rate relief from the city council but otherwise has no regular grant aid. It depends on income raised through membership subscriptions (currently £15 for a full member, £8 for a junior and £5 for a 'social' member); profit on its own productions; hiring the theatre to local groups; promoting the occasional professional touring production; bar sales and costume, scenery and equipment hire. In the year ended 30 April 1997, the Footlights Club productions (and related activities) produced income of about £36,000, of which £14,500 was transferred to the Grand Theatre Fund as a 'notional rental charge'. The Grand Theatre (lets, hiring, catering and bar) produced income of about £63,000.

During the three years ended 30 April 1997, over £100,000 was spent on refurbishment work. Grants from the Foundation for Sport and the Arts and from Lancaster City Council Heritage

Fund contributed £38,300 towards the cost of this work, the rest being found from the Grand Theatre Fund.

Its resident ghost has also lent a hand. In 1997 a television programme was made about the mysterious female figure which haunts the theatre.

The future

The Lancaster Footlights Club has established a niche role for the *Grand Theatre* within Lancaster arts provision. Jon Harris, Lancaster City Arts Officer, commented 'The theatre is constantly used and used by the community. Its productions attract a much broader audience base than either the *Nuffield* (a drama and dance space at Lancaster University) or the *Dukes Playhouse*.'

The club is now looking at how it can build on this community base and strengthen the relatively secure position which it has struggled so hard to achieve. All amateur groups have to constantly renew their membership, particularly amongst young people, to maintain the 'skill resource' on which their future depends. Amongst the possibilities being considered by the Lancaster Footlights Club is the addition of a small studio space which could be used for workshops and junior productions. They are hoping that the lottery fund will continue long enough to allow them time to decide how best to develop their 200-year-old theatre building before submitting an application.

Reference material

The Grand Theatre Lancaster: Two Centuries of Entertainment, Occasional Paper No. 11 produced by North-West Regional Studies, University of Lancaster (1982)

Key Points

- A small theatre which was never completely closed
- Turned down by the local authority for conversion to provide the civic theatre for Lancaster
- Given a successful new role by the Lancaster Footlights Club as its home and as a base for amateur productions
- Run by volunteers with no regular revenue support for the past forty seven years.
- Refurbished step-by-step as money could be made available

Type of operation:
Home for amateur dramatic company. Receiving venue for other amateur and some small-scale professional productions.
Ownership and management:
Owned and managed by Lancaster Footlights Club
Original architects:
Built in 1782 (architects unknown)
Current theatre reconstructed within shell of Georgian original:
1908 architects, Albert Winstanley
Listed:
Grade II
Uses:

1782–1841	*circuit theatre*
1841–84	*concert hall, lecture room and museum*
1884–1930	*theatre*
1930–51	*cinema with some live performance*
1951 continuing	*theatre*

Current capacity:
465

Hackney Empire, London

*'It was like visiting a favourite pub
with the very best of entertainment on offer'*

Angela Stern, Friends of Hackney Empire

Introduction

Every theatre has its own distinct character but few more so than the *Hackney Empire*. Writing in *Curtains !!!*, John Earl, former Director of The Theatres Trust describes it as 'a magnificent example of a turn-of-the-century variety house' and references its 'splendidly exuberant terracotta façade; marble and alabaster entrance hall; and opulent auditorium'. An appeal brochure issued by the Hackney Empire Preservation Trust uses more theatrical language to get across the impact which this theatre makes on the first-time visitor.

Entering the auditorium of the *Hackney Empire* is one of London's great architectural experiences ... a tiny box-office leads on to the foyer where Haydn and Mozart peer through the stained varnish of oil paintings. Beyond, dark passages and stairways belie the imminent thrill. Then, quite unexpectedly, an Aladdin's cave of space opens up. A spectacle in red and gold unfolds. The elaborate proscenium arch, crowned by two Moorish domes, towers over the stalls. Gothic masks grimace from the balconies, cherubs ogle sedate muses across the aisle, drawing the eye upwards through a riot of gilt stucco, towards a superbly ornate ceiling. Up in the Gods, the steeply tiered seats of the Gallery focus down on the stage, far below. In successive waves, the curve of the upper circle and the sweep of the dress circle cascade on to the stalls, articulating the outrageous spatial welcome that makes the *Hackney Empire* so special.

For many years, all this served as a mere backdrop to bingo. The doors only closed in 1986 when it had become apparent that the bingo operation could no longer sustain the building. The theatre was rescued by a group of actors and artists who had been working the clubs and pubs with a concept of entertainment which they called 'New Variety'. They were determined to bring the old *Empire* back to life and to fill it once again with a rich programme of variety – not as an anachronistic and nostalgic replica of a past form, but as contemporary popular entertainment.

Like the traditional phoenix, the *Hackney Empire* has recreated itself and has re-established its place in the London scene. It is once again a popular (and now increasingly fashionable) place to go for a good night out as well as a showcase for new artists and visiting companies. But, despite its recognised success, the theatre's grasp on financial security remains a tentative one. The management faces all the problems that confront companies seeking to promote quality live work while having to maintain and improve a one-hundred-year-old listed building (grade II*).

The first decades

The theatre was built for Oswald Stoll (later part of Stoll Moss) and designed by the prolific theatre architect Frank Matcham as one of the great palaces of variety. It was always seen as a Number 1 house on the Stoll Moss circuit and, over the years, brought many of the best known names in popular entertainment to London's East End audiences. Marie Lloyd, Charlie Chaplin, Lillie Langtry, Little Tich, Ella Shields, Dan Leno, Stan Laurel, Harry Lauder, George Robey, W C Fields, and George Formby all played the *Empire*.

When the theatre was built in 1901, one of Matcham's innovations was to install a Bioscope projection box at the rear of the dress circle enabling films to be shown as part of the variety bill on the opening night. From 1915 onwards, the theatre became a cinema on Sundays.

The rest of the time, live entertainment predominated

and continued into the 1950s. British comedians such as Tommy Trinder, Max Miller, and Tony Hancock were joined by international stars including Louis Armstrong.

As interest in variety declined, the theatre which was so perfectly designed for that form of entertainment, declined with it. The building closed as a theatre in February 1956, with a final music hall production entitled 'Thanks for the Memory' and, for a while, stood empty. It was saved from further decay when London's first independent television company, ATV, moved in. The entire stalls were boarded over to create a studio 'stage' and invited audiences sat in the dress circle to watch such shows as *Take Your Pick* and *Opportunity Knocks* being televised live from the *Empire*. But the company expanded fast and soon needed to find larger premises. After five years as a TV studio, the building was sold to Mecca in 1963 and given over to bingo. The front stall seats were reinstated while the raised flat-floored rear stalls area housed bingo tables. (This space is still unseated and is now used as an informal bar standing area.) The exuberant red and gold colour scheme actually dates from the Mecca period. When the auditorium was redecorated in 1978, the cream, green and gold colour scheme of the original was changed and the remaining gold leaf and many of the surviving decorative panels were painted over. The original canopy which ran along the exterior

of the building was also lost. That same year, the Department of the Environment listed the building (initially at grade II).

The story of the domes

The Matcham exterior had featured two massive terracotta domes, flanking a curved pediment topped by a statue of Euterpe, the Greek muse of instrumental music. Most of this structure had survived the second world war bombing which destroyed the Britannia (the public house which made up the corner of the theatre block), but years later was reported to be unstable. Mecca received a dangerous structures notice. Its response was to remove the entire skyline – the pediment and both domes – without seeking the consent which the building's listed status required (1979). This event served to focus attention on the *Hackney Empire* and proved to be one of the factors which led first to its sale and then to its reopening as a theatre.

For a while nothing was done. When challenged by the

The replacement statue of Euterpe is put into position. (*The Independent/Keith Dobney*)

local authorities, Mecca claimed that the cost of repair in terra-cotta would be too great and announced its intention to have glass-reinforced plastic facsimiles made. The ensuing dispute went to public inquiry. The Secretary of State for the Environment ruled that the domes should be reinstated in their original material, a decision which was greeted with delight both by the conservationists and by the then ailing manufacturers of terracotta detailing.

Following a long drawn-out enforcement action by Hackney Borough Council and the Historic Buildings Division of the Greater London Council (GLC), the domes were reinstated (in terracotta) by Mecca at an estimated cost of £250,000. The missing central figure was also replaced (with financial help from the Heritage of London Trust and of English Heritage). But by this time, the theatre had been already been reclaimed as a place of live entertainment.

In comes CAST

The key player in the *Empire*'s revival is theatre director, Roland Muldoon, who recognised the special quality of the theatre for live entertainment, led the rescue bid, got a programme underway, and then stayed on to run the theatre. During the 1960s he had formed the left-wing touring company CAST (Cartoon Architypical Slogan Theatre) and then set up CAST New Variety in response to what he saw as a growing need, amongst the younger, post-TV generation, for a good night out with live entertainment. Muldoon describes the 'New Variety' concept as 'like traditional variety, embracing all the disciplines of perform-ance art – *commedia dell'arte*, left wing, always entertaining, often challenging and sometimes plain dangerous'. In 1984, in the last year before its abolition, the GLC gave CAST what was for them a massive input of funding – £250,000 to be spent in one year – and this enabled a whole range of new artists to be promoted. The growing strength of the CAST operation helped convince Muldoon that the New Variety needed a more permanent home – a local, metropolitan and national venue for the new gener-ation of performers who were coming to prominence on the cabaret circuits. In a 1990 interview, he explained 'I believe quite sincerely that if there is a future for popular theatre in Britain, it must come from popular artists who learned their skills in alternative cabaret. Gradually we're moving out of the pubs, into the bigger venues, and I predict we'll go into the major ones.'

CAST New Variety had hoped to persuade the GLC to buy the *Hackney Empire* from Mecca (asking price £250,000) but before negotiations got underway the Government put a block on all GLC capital spending. Mecca then offered the

Roland Muldoon. (*Times Newspapers Limited*)

theatre to CAST for £1000. Although this may sound like a bargain, whoever bought the theatre would be responsible for reinstating the domes and English Heritage had made clear its intent to issue any new owner with an immediate order (in-curring a fine for every day of subsequent delay). CAST was advised to bide its time.

CAST had set up the Hackney Empire Preservation Trust (HEPT), to buy and repair the building, and Hackney New Variety, a non-profit distributing company to programme and manage the theatre. While negotiations were still continuing, Mecca closed the bingo operation (2 November 1986). Accord-ing to contemporary reports, a large team of volunteers moved into the building the following day and, to the amazement of the Mecca staff, started ripping out the bingo apparatus so that the stage, which lay hidden beneath false floors and redundant bingo electrics, could be cleared. Their intention was that the theatre would open again on 9 December – *Hackney Empire*'s eighty-fifth birthday. The two-and-a-half ton safety curtain had to be brought out of retirement, the false ceiling was tested, and lighting and sound equipment had to be installed. The theatre opened as planned.

Hackney New Variety stayed on to run shows in the theatre for the whole of the following year – even though no deal had been reached with Mecca. Finally it was agreed. Mecca would reinstate the domes and HEPT would buy the theatre for £150,000 – £50,000 by May 1988 and £100,000 by the next year. Even then there was a problem. If the initial payment was not made by the deadline HEPT would incur a penalty of

£50,000. The trust had managed to raise £25,000 from a public appeal by the time it reached the deadline and a loan was secured so that the purchase could be completed on time. The trust was enabled to purchase the lease in October of that year, by a grant from Hackney Borough Council (part of the 'planning gain' accruing from the Broadgate redevelopment).

In July 1989, the building's listed status was upgraded to grade II*, which gave it automatic eligibility for maintenance and restoration grants. Grants from English Heritage and from the European Regeneration Fund helped towards the cost of renovating the exterior of the building (including overhauling much of the roof) and restoring the stage grid. In 1995, the gallery, which had been left derelict for the previous forty years, was renovated with proceeds from a grant from the Baring Foundation. The renovation brought the seating capacity up to its present level of 1300 seats (with space for a further 200 standing.)

Variety returns to the Empire

When CAST and HEPT took on the *Hackney Empire*, they had only £10,000 in hand. During the first years the theatre was kept going with the support of volunteers, goodwill productions by the artists which CAST had launched and others who recognised the value of a theatre dedicated to popular entertainment. Bar sales and theatre lets (it proved popular as a film set and backdrop for commercials as well as for productions) made up the deficit.

With a neglected historic theatre to refurbish, a programme to run, and very little money to do either, HEPT decided it needed to expand. It bought a twenty-eight year lease on the adjacent public house for £35,000. The original Britannia pub had been destroyed and replaced in 1957/58, by the Samuel Pepys, a utilitarian structure of little architectural merit and, more to the point, a less than welcoming attitude to 'outsiders'. HEPT's intention in buying the pub was to provide a rendezvous facility so that the audience did not have to queue round the block while they waited to get into their seats. Though the move was described by some as 'completely bonkers', the new space enabled HEPT to open a cabaret bar (downstairs) and the *Lookout* theatre (small studio space, upstairs) in which to showcase new artists. The extended bar areas also brought in more income. (The pub currently makes £70,000 a year for the theatre.)

By the tenth anniversary of its reopening, the *Empire* was once again established as a variety venue. It had mounted a wideranging programme including black comedy and Jamaican farces, stand up comedy and new variety, drama, music, opera, Turkish productions, charity benefits and pantomimes. Amongst the many 'unknown' artists that the *Empire* has helped promote are John Hegley, Jo Brand, Julian Clary, Harry Enfield, Paul Merton, Felix Dexter, Lily Savage, and Ardol O'Hanlon. Stage shows have included: *The Long March*; *Black Heroes in the Hall of Fame*; *Sarafina*; the Almeida's *Hamlet* with Ralph Fiennes; and Warren Mitchell's *King Lear*. Clowning is seen as part of the variety programme. The *Empire* has mounted productions by Slava Polunin (*Snowshow*) as well as visits from Ra Ra Zoo and Circus Senso who became the backup for Cirque Du Soleil. Companies from many different countries have been invited to the *Empire* to present their work to London audiences. They include the Pan African Dance Ensemble; Ankara Art Theatre; Moldavian National Opera Company; Jamaican National Panto Company and the Market Theatre of Johannesburg with a production of *The Good Woman of Sharpeville* (based on Brecht's play).

Hackney Empire now receives revenue grants from the London Arts Board, the London Borough Grants Scheme, and the London Borough of Hackney. Together these three funders provide twenty-four per cent of the income for the theatre's £2 million operation. Ticket sales provide the bulk of the income. The theatre puts on mainly evening and late night shows with some matinées for family and school productions. Seat prices range from £2 to £12.50 (£1 to £5 in the *Lookout* theatre).

Incoming companies either pay a hire fee; a share of take (for example a 30/70 split for shows likely to sell well); or some mixture of the two. The theatre is also rented out to film crews making pop videos and feature films.

During 1997 and 1998, two six-week series of black music hall, *Nights out at the Empire,* were recorded at the theatre for transmission by Channel 4 TV. A third series is planned.

The lottery and 2001

When the National Lottery was announced in 1993, HEPT saw it as providing the chance to put in hand the major refurbishment which the theatre needed if it was to survive through to the next millennium.

A new company, Hackney Empire Limited, was formed to take over from the two existing organisations (HEPT and CAST New Variety) and applied for charitable status. It set out its artistic policy as follows:

The *Hackney Empire* aims to be the leading London theatre dedicated to the widest range of popular entertainment from music hall and variety through to today's new variety, dance, music, stand-up comedy, contemporary versions of

Shakespeare and travelling opera. The Theatre aims to build on its reputation as a notable, innovative, multi-cultural landmark feeding other art forms – cinema, TV, radio and recording. It also aims to allow new audiences and performers from no theatre going backgrounds to access Theatre and to provide a platform for developing art forms from different cultural traditions.

In October 1996, the Arts Council offered Hackney Empire Ltd a grant of £1.5 million towards the cost of a package of land acquisition, a feasibility study and a design competition. The resulting brief involved the full restoration of Matcham's amazing interior and associated circulation areas; the complete re-construction of the stage and backstage to provide facilities for larger and more frequent productions; the replacement of the Samuel Pepys pub on the corner of the block housing the theatre with a new building providing new pub and enhanced rendez-vous space, restaurant, small theatre, foyer, bar and lifts; and the construction of a further new building containing workshops, rehearsal studio, offices and gallery. Two sites were acquired to accommodate the proposed new buildings: one was the freehold of the Samuel Pepys for £400,000 (the theatre already had a leasehold agreement on this property) and a warehouse/office building just behind the theatre. The cost of the development was estimated at £30 million.

The design competition was launched in February 1997 by Doris Lockart Saatchi, an enthusiastic supporter of the *Hackney Empire* and a member of the board of the new company. Seeking a bold and contemporary design approach, the assessment panel selected a specially formed team led by Iraqi sisters, Homa and Sima Farjadi and Tim Ronalds Architects. The team submitted an ingenious design described as 'a lantern overlooking Town Hall Square, with a skin that glows, suggestive of the exotic and theatrical world within'. The plan was to phase the construction so that the main house would only be dark for ten months and the whole project would be completed in time for *Hackney Empire*'s centenary celebrations in 2001.

The *Hackney Empire* lottery bid was finally delivered to the Arts Council at the end of May 1998. By then, the projected cost had risen to nearly £40 million, of which the Arts Council was asked to contribute £28 million. The theatre had already raised £5 million, including a pledge of £200,000 from the Monument Trust and a campaign had been put in hand to raise the further £5 million needed to meet the 'partnership' element in the funding package. The artists who the *Empire* had helped to launch rallied to the theatre's support. An advertisement featur-ing Harry Enfield was run in fifty cinemas (courtesy of Pearl and Dean); a campaign featuring Jack Dee was sited on hoardings

(*John Earl*)

across London; and Griff Rhys Jones headed a charity auction. Full page advertisements appeared in the *Evening Standard* and *The Guardian* and mobile trucks travelled between *Hackney Empire* and the Arts Council carrying the appeal poster.

But by the middle of 1998, the initial bonanza of seemingly unlimited lottery funding was coming to an end. The Arts Council was looking at ways of allocating funding within a very much more restricted framework, and the ten English regional arts boards were each being asked to identify their priorities within the context of total capital funds of £60 million being available for each area over an eight-year period (1998–2006). The *Empire*'s response was to stress its national significance, in the hope that it would not be subjected to the limitations placed on the regional arts boards. But the money for national projects

(*John Earl*)

had already been earmarked. Even the combination of Roland Muldoon and the *Hackney Empire* could not hope to secure almost half London's available money for a single project. At the end of July 1998 it heard that the Arts Council of England had rejected the lottery bid.

Where now?

When these case studies went to press, the Arts Council's decision had only just been announced and the board of Hackney Empire Limited and its advisers were in the process of considering their options. While their plans for the 2001 celebrations now seem unlikely to be implemented in full, the project has raised a tremendous momentum of support which could well carry the theatre some way towards its target. The company now owns both the pub and the adjacent office/warehouse (both potential income generators) and probably has more money in its capital fund than has been spent on the building during the previous one-hundred-odd years of its life. The heading on the theatre's press release sets out their philosophy, 'Pick ourselves up, dust ourselves down and start all over again.'

Key Points

- Designed by Frank Matcham as a No.1 variety house for Oswald Stoll
- Exuberant architectural style now listed grade II*
- Closed as a theatre in 1956 but in continuous use for other purposes
- Reopened by CAST in 1986 on a shoe string as a home for 'New Variety'
- Developed a reputation for popular entertainment and multicultural productions
- Major redevelopment planned and lottery funding sought

Type of operation:
Receiving venue and 'New Variety' house
Ownership and management:
Owned and managed by Hackney Empire Limited
Original architect:
1901 Frank Matcham
Architects for current project:
Homa and Sima Farjadi and Tim Ronalds Architects
Listed:
Grade II*
Uses:

1901–56	*theatre*
1956–63	*TV studio*
1963–86	*bingo*
1986 continuing	*theatre*

Current capacity:
1300 (plus 200 standing)

Stephen Joseph Theatre, Scarborough

*'The culmination of a forty-year learning process
and a twenty-year dream'*

Alan Ayckbourn

Introduction

When, in 1955, Alan Ayckbourn first joined the *Stephen Joseph Theatre* in Scarborough it was based in two small rooms on the first floor of the local library. At the same time the *Odeon Cinema*, a striking Art Deco building in the centre of the town, was still filling its 1700-seat auditorium with a regular programme of films.

But by the late 1980s, the cinema stood empty. The theatre company had moved from the library to a redundant school but this space too was proving too cramped for its needs. Could one make a home for the other? A huge modernist cinema with an end-stage, proscenium format and double tier of fixed raked seating would seem to be an unlikely prospect for housing the best known 'theatre-in-the round' company in the country. But the building had potential both in terms of its town centre site and its generous interior spaces. Recognising this, the Stephen Joseph Theatre Company proceeded to negotiate the purchase, raise the necessary funding, take out much of the interior structure of the building and refurbish the rest; and, within the spaces created, to design and build its new home.

Most of the 'super cinemas' which survived were converted during the 1960s and 1970s to provide two or three separate auditoria. The purpose built multi-screen cinema complexes now spreading across the country, could soon drive some of these older 'multiplexes' out of business leaving the buildings which house them to find new roles. This case study looks at how one such cinema was successfully adapted to house a very different type of operation.

The first forty years

Stephen Joseph, son of actress Hermione Gingold and publisher Michael Joseph, discovered theatre-in-the round when travelling in America. After a long and unsuccessful search for a suitable space to create a theatre in this country, he arrived in Scarborough and, quite by chance, got into conversation with the librarian there who offered him a small area on the first floor of the public library.

Stephen Joseph built his theatre-in-the-round, set up a small company and began to put on plays. The young Alan Ayckbourn joined the company as an actor/stage-hand/technician and soon took on the additional jobs of writer, director and designer. He moved on to other work but maintained his links with the company and, in 1970, following the death of Stephen Joseph (at the early age of thirty-nine), returned to Scarborough to run the theatre.

The company remained at the *Library Theatre* until 1976, fitting its entire operation into two rooms. (The space still exists and is used for concerts.) Alternative accommodation was then found in the town's former grammar school. Though originally seen as a temporary solution, the company remained there for a further seventeen years, renewing the lease every two years, until the current owner, the Yorkshire Coast College, decided that it needed the space for its own activities.

During the years between the opening of the original theatre and the purchase of the *Odeon* building, the concept for the eventual theatre was being developed. In a booklet illustrating the *Odeon* project, Ayckbourn writes:

This theatre is a dream that has been with me as long as I can remember. For it was, of course, originally Stephen Joseph's dream; a permanent custom built theatre for Scarborough. I remember once, when he was ill, sitting in his bedroom over a whole weekend, helping him to make a card model of his 'dream' theatre to be built heaven knows where and Lord knows how or when; a theatre in the round (of course), an intimate, compact crucible where the essential elements of theatre – actor and audience – could be best brought to the point of spontaneous dramatic combustion. Exciting. Daring.

The new theatre is in many ways an expression of the philosophies of its two directors. To refer to it as two men's dreams could suggest an ephemeral and impractical quality at odds with the final product. Stephen Joseph spent years studying the form and working out how theatre-in-the-round might be presented most effectively. The size and shape of the stage; the positioning, height and number of seats; the exact inclination of the rake; the points of entrance and egress for the actors – all were meticulously calculated. The design principles were tested and refined through several hundred productions both in Scarborough and at the second theatre which Stephen Joseph established in the Midlands (the original *Victoria* in Stoke-on-Trent which, interestingly, was also housed in a converted cinema building).

The *Library Theatre* had given Ayckbourn his first opportunities as a writer and he was determined that the *Stephen Joseph Theatre* would continue to provide this role for others. About sixty per cent of the programme over the years has been new work. Revenue support from Yorkshire and Humberside Arts, Scarborough Borough Council and North Yorkshire County Council enabled the company to maintain this level of innovation. In the new, larger theatre, Ayckbourn knew that he would need to present a balanced programme so that a popular play could support a not so popular but equally worthy production. His 'ideal' was to have two auditoria, one of which could double as a cinema to broaden the appeal of the building.

The decision to leave the school building was not a sudden one. The company had been aware of the need to establish a new base for its operations for many years and Ayckbourn had been looking out for a possible site or building which could be developed in line with his plans. 'Thinking about possibilities', began to focus on the *Odeon Cinema* when it closed in 1987.

The Odeon?

The former *Odeon* occupies a prominent position, directly opposite the station and at the foot of the hill leading up the main shopping street to the sea front. It is not an easy building to miss. Its façades, blocks of black or white tiling set against the dark brown of the structural brickwork, stretch along two streets, with the glazed drum of the main entrance marking the corner where these streets meet. The building is also signposted by an art deco 'pylon' which the original owners managed to have erected in the middle of the road.

The cinema was opened in March 1936, designed by Cecil Clavering and Robert Bullivant of the Harry Weedon practice, seating 944 in the stalls and 765 in the circle – a total of 1709. Part of an impressive group of Modernist cinemas for Oscar Deutsch's Odeon chain, it was the only one to have retained the single auditorium in its original state.

By the end of the 1980s the cinema was closed and was rapidly falling into disrepair. An article published in *The Daily Telegraph* (27 May 1993) describes the theatre's proposed new home.

It would be dishonest to pretend that the heart lifts at the sight of the former *Odeon Cinema* in Scarborough. Built in 'streamlined modernist' style in 1936, its art deco style façade is grimy and chipped. Inside the cold, damp auditorium, dust gathers on the popcorn counter and the carpet rots in the central aisle.

Though rundown and neglected, the building had its supporters. Ayckbourn's plans for the *Odeon* involved the demolition of

(*Martine Hamilton Knight*)

much of the auditorium and for this, listed building consent was required. The report prepared for the Historic Buildings Advisory Committee of English Heritage concluded that, despite the unique interior, the building's grade II listing status and its principal interest lay in 'its external expression'. Having assessed the likelihood of any alternative users making sufficient money to reinstate the exterior, English Heritage came to the 'reluctant' conclusion that there were insufficient grounds for the application made by the Stephen Joseph Theatre Company to be 'called in' for a public inquiry. Consent was granted.

In 1989, Alan Ayckbourn, together with two partners, Viscount Downe (who lives near Scarborough), and Charles McCarthy (then head of the McCain G.B. frozen food group, a significant employer in the area) set up a company called 'The ADMirable Partnership' to buy the lease of the *Odeon*. The three partners bought the remaining forty-six year lease from Rank, negotiating the price down to £200,000 from the asking price of £300,000. Each of the partners put in £50,000 and the company raised a loan for the remaining amount. Scarborough Borough Council gave a grant of £50,000 towards the cost of feasibility studies and agreed to extend the lease to

ninety-nine years. The initial studies showed that something in the region of £4 million would be needed. Unable to envisage raising this figure in a country then heading into recession, the partnership bided its time and concentrated on planning the 'ideal' theatre.

Working with the architects

Henry Osbourne of Osbourne Christmas Architects was appointed to develop the concept, working in close association with Alan Ayckbourn to establish exactly what was needed, how it could best be provided, and how it could be fitted within the structure of the existing building. A theatre consultant was appointed to advise on the technical aspects of the design and all the theatre staff were encouraged to involve themselves in the detailed design work. The architects were concerned to establish the practicalities of the theatre's operation, particularly factors

(Shepherd Design Ltd)

relating to the production budget constraints. Changing from one production to another to maximise the summer season audience was an expensive operation in the school based theatre as extra staff had to be hired in at peak rates.

While substantial additional space was needed for a second auditorium and radically improved audience and production facilities, the 'tightness' of the original theatre-in-the-round was seen as one of its main strengths. Alan Ayckbourn was determined not to lose the sense of immediacy and intimacy which the audience had experienced in the two previous theatres. He agreed to one more row being added to the theatre-in-the-round format (increasing the number of rows from five in the existing theatre to six in the new theatre and the potential capacity from 305 to 400 seats respectively).

Osbourne Christmas took the project as far as the detailed design stage. By then the cost had been established at £4.35 million. A separate company was formed 'The Scarborough Theatre Development Trust' to get the project on its way.

Money and building

The first additional money came through a freak accident. When fire in the telephone exchange destroyed 23,000 local phone lines, BT, as a goodwill gesture, gave £250,000 to a trust set up by Scarborough Borough Council for 'good causes in the town'. The council handed the money over to the theatre.

The main appeal was launched in June 1993. Several large companies promised contributions, the Foundation for Sport and the Arts agreed a contribution of £500,000 'to assist with the relocation to the *Odeon Cinema*', Ayckbourn gave £400,000, and McCarthy put in £250,000. With £1.9 million in the bank or pledged, the Scarborough Theatre Trust decided to go ahead with the first stage of the building work.

The procurement route was an unusual one for an arts development. Once planning permission had been secured on the basis of the Osbourne Christmas design, the trust approached the Shepherd Company to carry out an evaluation of the scheme for development and construction under a design-and-build form of contract. The company offered a fixed price for the job and undertook to finish it within a tight construction period. Though people have commented that some of the detailing suffered from this method of working, the trust obtained remarkable value for its money (the final cost of the two theatres and supporting accommodation was £5.25 million) and each stage of the building work was completed by the target date.

The timing, fortuitously, coincided with the introduction of the National Lottery. The trust had planned to bring the first phase into operation and then stop work while it raised further funding (plans had been drawn up to enable the studio/cinema to function independently). In the event, an Arts Council of England (ACE) lottery grant of £1.48 million enabled the whole conversion to be carried out as a single contract. The lottery contribution also helped secure a £495,000 grant from EC5b – European money available for projects aimed at the regeneration of the local economy.

Shortly before the theatre opened, two further ACE lottery awards were announced – £98,000 towards the cost of purchasing and refurbishing a warehouse for a costume and props storehouse and £99,000 towards the cost of new lighting and sound equipment for the *Stephen Joseph Theatre*.

How the building was converted

The basic brief was for two auditoria to be fitted into the shell of the cinema space, sharing support facilities. The foyer (including the restaurant and bar areas) and the exterior of the building were to be reinstated to their original 1936 condition.

The solution was an ingenious one. The upper floor of the original cinema foyer had led into the back of the circle. In the new theatre, the central rear section of this circle was retained to form the auditorium for the new 200-seat studio/cinema space, with the stage being built where the old front circle seats had been. The side sections of the original cinema circle were closed off to create circulation routes through the building. The stalls seating and screen/proscenium arch of the former cinema were removed to create sufficient space for the theatre-in-the-round. An atrium was constructed between the two auditoria, bringing light and air into the core of the building. Dressing-rooms and offices (often rather miserable spaces even in some new theatre buildings) look onto a conservatory which was created within this atrium. A bridge crosses the atrium space, providing a transit between the old and the new and forming a focal circulation and meeting point. The 'green room' is placed at the base of the atrium, serving as a place of relaxation not only for performers but for everybody who works in the building.

While this solution created two distinct auditoria, pleasant working spaces and good bar, foyer and circulation areas, it also produced the problem of servicing upper-level stage areas. (The design resulted in the theatre-in-the-round stage being at first-floor level with stage of the studio space one level higher.) The 'backstage' had to be housed 'below stage'. With the theatre-in-the-round, this proved to be an advantage as it provided space for an hydraulic lift to be installed. The lift takes the whole of the stage area down into the workshop which is situated at street level. Access to the studio space is less satisfactorily managed with the get-in door positioned halfway up the outside of the building. Conservation requirements prevented any major structural changes being made to incorporate lifting gear so a crane has to be hired and road closure negotiated when visiting companies bring large sets into the studio space.

Technical provision

The brief and the constraints of the existing building led the consultants to devise technically innovative solutions. The most significant single service element is the stage lift system. This consists of a steel platform extending over the whole stage area which is powered to service levels below the auditorium by means of a rack and pinion drive system, located on the main shaft columns. A second lift, which can be independently operated, moves the slip stages, or wagons, which sit on top of the lift platform, 'winching' them off laterally into the rehearsal room and workshops at one level or into storage at the level below. The lift system enables sets to be pre-made on wagons and held in storage, saving on the labour costs incurred when sets are changed between productions.

Another 'first' for a British theatre is the use of a tensile wire 'trampoline' lighting grid which extends over the whole theatre-in-the-round auditorium. This grid enables lanterns to be mounted close to the plane of the wire and project through it, eliminating any 'shadowing' effects. The lighting technicians can walk over the entire grid to position lanterns, while leaving the stage and seating levels free for others in the production team. This enables the technicians to work concurrently in preparing shows, resulting in much shorter turn-around times for the theatre's varied programme.

The seating is arranged in four blocks (creating a square rather than a circle) and is designed to provide a high degree of flexibility. The first three rows of seating in each of the four blocks can be removed in units of two and three seats, enabling the stage to be extended in any direction.

The current operation

The new *Stephen Joseph Theatre* opened in April 1996 with a newly written version of Alan Ayckbourn's and Andrew Lloyd Webber's musical *By Jeeves* with the season which followed featuring plays by Alan Bennett (*Forty Years On*) and Michael Frayn (*Wild Honey*), a varied programme of film, as well as writers' 'platforms', workshops, exhibitions, music and education activities.

The theatre hit the national media again just one year later, firstly when Scarborough Council was split on whether or not to grant the company a further £50,000 a year and again in March 1997 under the headline 'Stephen Joseph Facing Closure' (*The Stage*), when North Yorkshire County Council took the decision to withdraw the revenue support it was giving to drama throughout the county (threatening the theatre's matching funding package). After an intense campaign the matter was resolved and the theatre's funding requirements met.

The new operation currently employs some seventy people, the cost of which accounts for some two thirds of the theatre's total budget of £1.5 million. Over sixty of these are theatre and production staff. In the year ended March 1997, the theatre earned just under half its operating costs (£667,904). The operation was subsidised by The Arts Council of England (£325,000 including part of a special lottery grant to support the company during the first three years in the new building); Yorkshire and Humberside Arts (£236,200); Scarborough Borough Council (£141,000); and North Yorkshire County Council (£70,500). This £772,500 compares with the £300,000 a year which the company received in revenue support when it was based in the school theatre.

The new *Stephen Joseph Theatre* represents a tremendous leap in scale for the theatre. New and larger premises change the way

The old upper circle, adapted to provide a studio theatre/cinema space. (*Martine Hamilton Knight*)

an organisation operates and some find it difficult to make the necessary adjustments. Alan Ayckbourn's company already seems very much at home in its converted cinema, a credit, perhaps, to the quality of thought which went into the preparation.

Notes on other venues

The two best known theatres-in-the-round in the UK are the purpose-built *New Victoria Theatre* in Newcastle-under-Lyne (a 600-seat theatre created by Peter Cheeseman in accordance with the principles developed by Stephen Joseph) and the *Royal Exchange Theatre* in Manchester (a free-standing module built within the interior of Manchester's former *Cotton Exchange* seating 750 in three tiers of circles – currently being rebuilt and improved after being damaged by the IRA bombing of central Manchester. The *Royal Exchange* can also be used in a thrust stage format.)

Live venues currently operating in former cinemas include the *Horsham Arts Centre* (formerly the *Capitol Cinema*). The auditorium was converted to provide a small end stage theatre, preserving the proscenium end while cutting off the rear stalls and balcony to create spaces for other uses.

Source material

Building Study, *Architects' Journal*, 1/8 August 1996
Scarborough Evening News: Opening Night Colour Supplement Special, 18 April 1996

Key Points

- An established producing company moved into a 1930's cinema
- Proposed theatre use persuaded the local authority to give consent to major alterations being made to a listed building
- Design evolved from many years of planning
- Close consultation between the architects and the theatre staff helped solve production problems
- Innovative technology installed to service a stage at first-floor level

Type of operation:
Producing company (mainly 'theatre-in-the-round') using second space as a receiving venue (small-scale productions) and cinema
Ownership and management:
Owned by Scarborough Town Council and leased to the Scarborough Theatre Management Trust
Original architects:
1936 Harry Weedon practice
Architects for 1995/96 conversion/refurbishment:
Osbourne Christmas
Listed:
Grade II
Uses:

1938–88	*cinema*
1989	*lease bought for conversion to theatre but building remained closed until work started in 1994*
1996 continuing	*theatre*

Current capacity:

Theatre-in-the-round	400
Cinema/Studio	165

Alhambra Theatre, Bradford

The theatre whose site was once earmarked for a car park is now an integral part of Bradford's economic development strategy

Introduction

The *Alhambra* is one of the few theatres featured in these studies which never closed (except for refurbishment) though for many years its future hung in the balance. The revival of the theatre's fortunes goes hand in hand with the revival of Bradford itself.

Bradford was the centre of the Yorkshire wool trade and, with its stock of fine Victorian buildings, was one of the wealthiest cities in Britain. By the middle of this century it was rapidly becoming one of the poorest. With its mills standing empty, its economy in decline and its population falling, Bradford City Council took the decision to invest in tourism. Despite widely expressed scepticism, a few years later the city was celebrating winning the English Tourist Board's award for the fastest growing tourist destination. It had succeeded in placing Bradford firmly on the tourist circuit.

Leisure played an important part in this transformation. One of the city's initial achievements was to attract the Science Museum to base its proposed National Museum of Photography, Film and Television in Bradford. This was the first of the regional 'outposts' to be established by the big London-based national museums. The refurbishment of *St George's Hall* (for music) was the next major investment, soon to be followed by the modernisation and expansion of the *Alhambra* theatre.

A policy statement issued by The Bradford Economic Development Unit in 1994 sets out the city council's intent. 'The development of a highly successful tourism industry has done much to restore pride and confidence to Bradford. Our Commitment is to continue nurturing that industry to see it develop and grow.'

This promise has been honoured. Today the *Alhambra* theatre and studio, together with the restored *St George's Hall*, are seen as having a key role in the city's economy. They are managed directly by the Recreation Division of the City of Bradford Metropolitan District Council to ensure that they continue to contribute towards the city's cultural and recreational life.

The route was not without its problems. A period of some twenty years elapsed between the fading of the *Alhambra*'s original glory and the establishment of the restored and refurbished theatre as a successful and viable operation.

A brief history

The story of the *Alhambra* starts with a patch of waste ground in the centre of Bradford, the site of warehouses and a brewery demolished as part of an early road improvement scheme. The land was purchased by Francis Laidler, a Bradford businessman turned impresario who already had a share in the *Princes Theatre*, built in 1876 and one of four successful theatres then operating in the city. The *Alhambra* was the largest and grandest of all Bradford's theatres. It was the first to be illuminated by electric lighting and carpeted throughout and the cantilevered circle ensured that every seat in the house had an uninterrupted view of the stage. The *Alhambra* cost £20,000 to build, seated 1800 and opened in March 1914, operating as a variety house staging two shows nightly. Laidler built up a reputation for high quality shows and for pantomime, which served to draw successive generations of children into the theatre. He died in 1954 at the age of eighty-eight but was succeeded by his second wife who continued to run the theatre for a further ten years. On her retirement in September 1964, a meeting of the principal shareholders agreed that the *Alhambra* should go into voluntary liquidation. Before announcing this decision they secured the agreement of Bradford City Council to buy the theatre (for £78,000) and lease it to Bradford Alhambra Ltd, a newly formed company directed by Rowland Hill who had been Laidler's right hand man for most of his career. Hill managed to keep the doors open until he retired in 1974. This continuity of management took the theatre through its most vulnerable years and effectively saved it from demolition.

Its future in the balance

During this period, the large variety theatres were all experiencing problems and the *Alhambra* was no exception. While the leasehold agreement gave Bradford City Council both a rental income and a share of the net profit, it also required the council to underwrite any losses. As the regular profits of the initial few years of ownership changed to regular losses, doubts began to be expressed about the future viability of the theatre.

The *Princes Theatre* had been demolished in 1961 as part of the first stage in a major redevelopment of the city centre. A block containing commercial offices was to be built (designed by architects Richard Seifert and Partners) in conjunction with work on a section of the new Civic ring road and was to contain a replacement theatre. The *Alhambra* was scheduled for demolition: its site earmarked for a car park.

By 1969, the shell of the new *Princes Theatre* was complete – 'a spanking new 1000-seater complete with crescent foyer, raked auditorium, skeleton stage, and air conditioning, just waiting to be fitted with seats, lights and revolve'. (*Plays and Players*, August 1971)

In 1972, the city council commissioned theatre consultant, John Wyckham, to report on the work needed to complete the *Princes Theatre*. He recommended that a number of quite major alterations would be required before it could be brought into operation. These included redesigning the auditorium; the main entrance foyer and upper foyers and, if possible, the fly-tower.

Times and tastes were already changing and the *Alhambra*, with its rich interior decoration and its three exterior domes which had long been a feature of Bradford's city centre landscape, looked an increasingly attractive alternative to the more bland exterior and plain auditorium of the *Princes Theatre*, encased as it was in a commercial office block. By 1973 the city council had decided that the *Alhambra* was the better bet. But money was in very short supply, audiences were dwindling and nobody could be found to invest in either building – one stood empty and uncompleted, the other struggled on.

It was not until 1980 that the city council finally got to grips with the problem of what to do with the *Princes Theatre* when it persuaded the Science Museum that Bradford's empty theatre shell was the right building to house the National Museum of Photography. That same year, the council also put in hand the renovation of the *St George's Hall* at a cost of £2.5 million.

Two years later, with the leisure/tourism investment policy already beginning to show dividends, the city commissioned the architectural practice of RHWL (Renton Howard Wood Levin) to explore the potential offered by the *Alhambra* and to establish the likely refurbishment cost.

Is there a future for the building?

The original 1914 theatre building had changed very little over the decades of use. Though the auditorium was a very fine one, it was let down by poor stage, back-stage and ancillary accommodation and minimal audience facilities.

RHWL's feasibility study showed that 'by selective surgery and the construction of extensive new additions, this grade II listed building could meet not just the expectations of late-twentieth-century audiences, but also the requirements of performers and the aspirations of the council to ensure the highest possible degree of commercial viability'.

What the report proposed was an ambitious venture which was obviously not going to be achieved on a low budget. The auditorium required careful handling in order to install new ventilation and sound and light systems while retaining the integrity of the ornate plasterwork and decorative murals. Extensive rebuilding work had to be carried out in very constricted working conditions and the existing structure needed to be restored and strengthened. The original *Alhambra*, though opulent in appearance, had been built very quickly to take advantage of the late Edwardian theatre boom years. In the event, the contractors found that domes had to be supported on hydraulic jacks until the new building work had been created to carry their weight.

The adjacent *Majestic* cinema needed to be purchased to enable the stage and backstage areas to be extended and rehearsal space provided. The front-of-house improvements and stage extension could only be achieved by narrowing one of the roads (creating a one way street).

Bradford City Council faced up to the challenge and set out to find the money. In February 1984 a top level, all party delegation went to Brussels where the enthusiastic support of the West Yorkshire Euro MP, Barry Seal, made sure that they met the 'right people'. They succeeded in securing an EEC grant of £2.1 million towards the cost of the project.

The refurbishment project

RHWL aimed to 'retain all that was best in the existing theatre' while replacing areas which were sub-standard or redundant.

The exterior is now a mixture of the old and the new, with the modern additions complementing but in no way copying, the refurbished Edwardian theatre structure. The three famous domes were retained, with the forward rotunda housing a new glazed grand staircase enabling the audience to be seen making its way around the building. The old street access was replaced by a spacious new entrance area with new foyers at three levels, providing food, relaxation and occasional daytime entertainment.

The auditorium itself was refurbished and redecorated in a range of gilts and shades of warm reds, with white and blues highlighting the tier fronts and proscenium boxes. The surfaces conceal the technical upgrading, with boxes and control rooms inserted at the rear, reducing the seating capacity but creating a greater sense of intimacy within what is now a 1500-seat auditorium. Provision was made for those with disabilities with removable seats providing wheelchair positions; a level access route from the street through to the Pit Bar and stalls; and designated WCs.

The stage area was doubled in depth and a completely new fly-tower was constructed. Bradford had planned to attract one of the national dance companies to move its operational base to the *Alhambra*. Though these plans did not materialise, dance continued to be seen as a key element in the programme and special provision was made for this use. The stage has a flat, lightly sprung floor and good wing space to allow for 'run-offs'. The orchestra pit was enlarged (in two sections) and a full-sized rehearsal space created. A large scenery lift was installed giving access to the stage direct from the street.

The original backstage accommodation was totally re-planned and re-equipped, and a new extension built over three levels to provide additional changing rooms, wardrobe, assembly area and get-in. An existing space within the old *Majestic* cinema, was transformed to provide a 200-seat auditorium (250 when standing) for smaller-scale musical and theatrical performances, community functions and some commercial lets. This studio space is also used by visiting dance companies and is fitted with a sprung floor and equipped as a dance warm-up, teaching and education facility.

The refurbishment and building work was completed in May 1986 at a total cost of £8.2 million.

Re-establishing the theatre operation

Though audiences returned in May 1986, the official gala opening of the newly refurbished theatre took place in the October when Jaques Delors, then President of the Commission of the European Communities, was there to mark the occasion. True to its traditions, the *Alhambra*'s first season featured a wide range of productions including the Northern Ballet's *Nutcracker* starring Rudolph Nureyev; *Jesus Christ Superstar*; *Murder on the Nile*; *The Sound of Music*; Tommy Steele; *The Lion, the Witch and the Wardrobe* and Ballet Rambert.

The building soon proved to be a tourist attraction in its own right. During the first three years after the opening, 25,000 visitors came to its public open days. They were given a tour of the theatre, shown an audio-visual of its history and were taken through the making of a production from get-in to performance – complete with a demonstration of lighting and sound effects.

The first administrator, Peter Tod, got the new venue off to a good start by insisting on and securing high quality productions with tours by the London Festival Ballet, the Royal Shakespeare Company and the National Theatre. The *Alhambra* was putting itself on the arts map and in 1992 its second administrator, Anamaria Willis, won the Martini regional theatre award for 'the most outstanding contribution to theatrical life'. As well as the traditional pantomime and community projects such as the Bradford Festival, audiences had been presented with productions by the Nederlands Dans Theater, the Maly Theatre of St Petersburg performing in Russian and Ariane Mnouchkine's *Les Atrides* (mounted by the *Alhambra* in an abandoned wool mill). Roger Lancaster, Yorkshire and Humberside Arts Director, was quoted in a local newspaper report – 'The *Alhambra* has been a role model for what regional theatres can achieve'.

While the theatre had demonstrated that it could be a success in creative terms, its management appeared to have a less certain grasp of the financial costs which this policy incurred. The recession was biting into disposable incomes and audiences were falling at the same time as the costs of providing an innovative and artistically adventurous programme were rising. An article in the *Daily Telegraph* (12 December 1992) quoted Ms Willis, 'Not all the risks we have taken have come off and, worst of all, the sure fire hits which we trusted to bankroll our adventures have not achieved the audiences we expected.' By the end of 1992, the *Alhambra* was hitting headlines again – it had an overspend of nearly £2 million.

Following a formal inquiry, the city council tightened its controls. The management responsibilities were placed directly in the hands of the council's head of recreation (who had the final say on what product was bought) and arrangements were made for the £2 million overspend to be paid back over a seven year period. Twenty staff were made redundant. Those who remained were faced with the enormous task of re-establishing the theatre operation and running it for £1,250,000 a year less than had been spent in the previous two years. With the help

(RHWL/Martin Charles)

(Alhambra Theatre/Guzelian Photography)

of some savings in other parts of the recreation services budget and very careful management, the £2 million debt was paid back ahead of schedule in 1996. In the same year, a new general manager, John Botteley, was appointed (though overall responsibility remained with departmental head).

The Alhambra today

The *Alhambra* continues to be managed by the city council as one of a group of seven venues. These include the *St George's Hall*; the *King's Hall and Winter Gardens* at Ilkley; the *Bingley Arts Centre* and the *Victoria Hall* in Saltaire. The group operates as 'Bradford Theatres' and is managed as a financial entity with staff being moved from one venue to another as required. The whole operation has a turnover of £6.5 million a year and receives an annual subsidy of £2 million. The subsidy includes debt repayments of £1 million (against borrowings for capital work) and a fixed contribution to the council's overheads. The general manager estimates that the actual operational subsidy for the seven venues is something in the region of £700,000 a year. They all operate as receiving venues though the *Alhambra* has recently set up a TIE (Theatre-in-Education) team which produces its own work at a cost of £100,000 per year. Ongoing repairs and maintenance are undertaken by Bradford Theatres to a planned programme. For major works bids have to be made to the council's overall capital programme.

Though most local authorities have handed their theatres over to specially formed trusts, John Botteley sees advantages to being part of a larger organisation. Within Bradford Theatres, the inevitable ups and downs in the financial success of different events tend to balance each other out, while the £21 million budget for the Recreation Services Department as a whole provides flexibility, with savings from one area being used to help another. The theatre also has access to professional and support services.

The first two administrators brought a wide range of different types and styles of production to the refurbished theatre. More recently, the *Alhambra* sought to concentrate on what it is best suited to do and has, to some extent, looked to its origins as a variety house for a successful model. The strength of its current programming lies in its role as a receiving house for large-scale musicals – such as the Cameron Mackintosh and Andrew Lloyd Webber productions. The musicals have long runs (in 1998 *Les Misérables* was booked in for twelve weeks) and play to sixty to eighty-five per cent capacity audiences drawn from a very large catchment area. A potential audience of six-and-a-half million lives within an hour's drive or train journey of the theatre. The

pantomime for which the *Alhambra* has long been famous remains the mainstay of its winter programme running for seven-and-a-half weeks and playing to seventy-five per cent capacity, earning between £800,000 and £1 million per season. Visits from the Birmingham Royal Ballet and the Northern Ballet Theatre account for a further three weeks. The *Alhambra* also hosts the larger 'set piece' drama productions toured by the national companies.

The studio theatre hosts one hundred events a year. When the planned improvements are completed, the aim is to programme this space to attract a number of regular but distinct audiences. This 'stranding' policy already works well at the *St George's Hall* where the audiences for classical, rock, popular and Asian music each identify the venue as serving their individual interests.

Continuing development

The *Alhambra* still looks good. The theatre has been well maintained and functions effectively. John Botteley describes it as 'an absolutely beautiful building to work in'. But twelve years on, several areas now need further investment. The 1986 refurbishment made some improvements to accessibility within the old building but more work is needed to meet current standards. Recent changes in the ownership of other parts of the 'block' in which the theatre is sited and a related development deal have enabled the theatre to acquire additional office space which will be used to house the education and development teams. This, in turn, will free-up space which was originally linked to the Studio theatre and enable this area to be redeveloped to house the TIE company, extending the scope of work which can be shown. The third area for which money will have to be found in the near future is the exterior of the building. The white terracotta facing requires cleaning and the exterior repainting – at an estimated cost in excess of £50,000.

The area surrounding the theatre is also changing. The nearby National Museum of Photography is currently being improved and extended by twenty-five per cent. The addition of a new five-storey atrium to the front of the building will bring the museum entrance physically closer to that of the *Alhambra* and the theatre should benefit from the increased number of visitors attracted to the area. Other live entertainment venues (pub theatre and music) are scheduled to open nearby, both in the block of which the *Alhambra* forms a part and in the adjacent *Odeon Cinema* (until recently used for bingo).

Bradford is continuing to extend its leisure and tourism opportunities and night life with the *Alhambra* as the focal point.

Reference theatres

The 'top five' venues for receiving large-scale musicals in England are the *Alhambra*, Bradford; the *Bristol Hippodrome*; the *Birmingham Hippodrome*; the *Mayflower* in Southampton and the two Apollo-owned Manchester theatres (the *Palace* and the *Opera House*) – plus the *Edinburgh Playhouse* in Scotland

Live performance venues still owned and managed by local authorities include two large theatres – the *New Theatre* in Hull and the *Sunderland Empire*; the *Hexagon*, Reading; the *Orchard Theatre*, Dartford; and the *Cambridge Corn Exchange*.

A number of Victorian and Edwardian theatres have been the subject of major refurbishment projects in which the foyer, stage and/or backstage areas were substantially altered or rebuilt. Those featured in these case studies are the *Palace Theatre*, Manchester; the *Festival Theatre*, Edinburgh; and the *Sheffield Lyceum*.

Source material

Domes of Delight the history of the Bradford *Alhambra* written by Peter Holdsworth. Published by Bradford Libraries and Information Service in 1989
Reports by the architects (RHWL) and the contractors (Higgs and Hill plc) issued as part of an information pack produced at the time of the theatre's reopening

The glazed grand staircase.
(*RHWL/Roger Pearson*)

Key Points

- The *Alhambra* retained the affection of local people both as a building and as a venue
- The theatre had been kept alive through the difficult years of the 1960s when many others closed
- The local authority had the determination to face up to problems and see the project through
- Feasibility studies were commissioned to look both at the need for the *Alhambra* (against other venues) and to establish what investment would be required
- From the outset, the refurbished *Alhambra* was designed to complement rather than compete with the Leeds theatres
- The local authority assessed the overall economic value of live theatre provision to the city rather than looking at a straight income/expenditure account for the single venue

Type of operation:
Receiving venue with TIE company and studio space
Ownership and management:
Owned and managed by Bradford City Council
Original architects:
1914 Chadwick and Watson
Architects for refurbishment:
1985 RHWL
Listed:
Grade II
Uses:
Continuous *theatre*
Current capacity:
Main theatre 1500
Studio 200

Tyne Theatre & Opera House, Newcastle upon Tyne

'Listing is no more than a first line of protection — it certainly does not ensure preservation in an appropriate beneficial use'

John Earl, former Director of The Theatres Trust

Introduction

The *Tyne* is one of the oldest remaining theatres in the country. It was built in 1867 and designed to provide Victorian audiences with the splendour and spectacle which they so enjoyed. The theatre is one of the few to carry a grade I listing.

But the *Tyne* is Newcastle's second theatre. Much of the major touring product and all the available local authority subsidy is directed towards the *Theatre Royal*. Its fine 1837 classical exterior and Matcham auditorium (rebuilt in 1901) provide an excellent setting for opera, dance and drama. More significantly, the *Theatre Royal* is able to seat 1350 while the *Tyne*'s capacity is only 1100. The *Royal* also has a larger stage and better backstage provision. Its predominance poses a problem. The *Tyne* is too precious a building to demolish and its unique features must be preserved but it is a theatre which, for the best part of this century, has had difficulty establishing a role within the city.

This case study cannot be presented as a success story. As this publication goes to press the theatre's future is once again uncertain. But strategies were found to refurbish the theatre and keep it open as a live performance venue for over twenty years.

The story of the *Tyne Theatre* involves a number of players, individuals and organisations, each having had a role in the shaping of events. What follows is a chronicle of those events. It does not purport to offer the definitive version or to provide all the details. Many of those involved will have their own versions of what happened and who, exactly, was responsible for the successes and the failures.

The Tyne Theatre

The *Tyne Theatre* is situated in Westgate Street, in a central, but rather run down, area of Newcastle a few minutes walk from the main station. Its exterior, with its three-storey brick and stone façade, tends to merge into the rest of the street. Were it not for the placards announcing current and future productions, many people would pass the building by without even realising that it is a theatre. Once inside, however, its significance is apparent. The blue, cream and gold auditorium is elaborately decorated with three horseshoe-shaped balconies sweeping round to meet the tiers of boxes which stand either side of the richly framed arch of the proscenium. There is an unusual and very beautiful circular panelled ceiling which is tilted slightly towards the gallery. This construction, together with the fact that the auditorium is lined throughout with timber, is thought to account for the theatre's excellent acoustics. The design is the work of architect William Parnell, his only theatre. The inspiration for the Italianate design may well have come from the owner himself, Tyneside industrialist Joseph Cowen, who had close links with Italy (he was a friend of Garibaldi) and with the theatres there.

The building's grade I listing relates not only to its fine auditorium but, as importantly, to the fact that the theatre has retained a unique set of wooden Victorian understage machinery. The *Tyne* was originally designed to present spectacular musical entertainment. One production featured the sinking of the Spanish Armada, another staged the Grand National with real horses and water jumps (the lead horse was played by an actual National winner). Storms raged, earthquakes thundered, caverns appeared and disappeared and scenes changed with amazing speed. All this was achieved by means of an intricate network of machinery which went deep under the stage. Four lift platforms, or bridges, spanned the entire width of the twenty-eight-foot stage, enabling whole sets to be pre-assembled below ground level and then winched into position using ten-foot gear wheels. There was a network of smaller lifts and trapdoors, the facility to flood the stage with one thousand gallons of water, and a thunder run.

The spectacle fades

But audiences and fashions change. In 1919, unable to meet the competition from other venues, the theatre was forced to close. Later the same year, it was bought by Oswald Stoll and reopened as a cinema, the *Stoll Picture Theatre*. Nothing was cleared out and no major structural alterations were made. The only additions were a screen across the stage and a projection box added to the rear of the upper circle.

The cinema operated successfully for several decades. When interest began to decline, the *Stoll* tried to keep going by showing a succession of 'adult' films giving the once impressive building the reputation of being seedy and run-down. At some point, the interior was painted black, totally obliterating the character of the fine auditorium with its gilded detailing.

A home for amateur operatics

The cinema use finally came to an end in 1974 and the building stood empty once again. This time, a group of amateur players sought to lease the property so that they could reopen it as 'a home for the musical'. They eventually persuaded Stoll Theatres Corporation to let them have the building for three years at a nominal rent and for a further twenty-five years at a commercial rent.

An initial loan of £6000 from Tyne & Wear County Council enabled the team of volunteers to start the cleaning and restoration work. It was when they were clearing out the theatre that the stage machinery was discovered beneath a pile of junk and debris where it had lain virtually intact for sixty years. The whole structure was carefully excavated and meticulously renovated by former geology student Dr David Wilmore who, through his work on this theatre, has since become a leading authority on nineteenth-century stage equipment.

The group found that there was a great deal of work to be done just to bring the theatre back into operation. It took three years. In 1977, the building was reopened under the management of an independent, registered charitable trust The New Tyne Theatre and Opera House Company Limited. Each of the trust's 400 members had one share. Its chairman was initially Jack Dixon, who made his living from a small electrical contracting business on Tyneside but found his entertainment by singing in the group's musical productions. He soon became the theatre manager and took charge of the whole operation, with Councillor Danny Marshall taking over as Chairman.

Work on the restoration proceeded steadily, helped by grants from Tyne and Wear County Council and from English Heritage. Much of it was carried out by the ordinary members of the company, who included professionals in appropriate areas, supplemented by the Government's Manpower Services Commission training and employment schemes. The auditorium was restored and the seating renewed, the theatre was rewired and a new lighting board installed. The foyers and bars were refurbished, new escape stairs were added and backstage access improved, a wardrobe department and new rehearsal rooms were created and the dressing-rooms modernised. In 1985 further dressing-rooms and rehearsal rooms were added and the theatre roof was renewed with the help of a major capital grant.

The company appointed a nucleus of professional staff to administer and operate the theatre but every aspect of the productions was carried out by the amateur team: scenery construction and painting; properties; costumes; and lighting as well as acting, singing and dancing. Other members ran the front of house, sold programmes and served in the bars. Once established, the company also ran a youth stage school. Between 1977, when the theatre reopened, and the end of 1985, more than seventy musicals had been staged.

This period in the *Tyne*'s history, has often been presented as the story of how an amateur operatic society secured its own theatre by putting on shows and, through hard work and determination, managed to bring in the income to keep the whole operation going. It is only a part of the story. Putting on shows rarely raises sufficient income to run a 1100-seat theatre. Even amateur productions cost money to mount with sets to be built, costumes to be hired, orchestras to be paid as well as advertising, heating, lighting and other running costs. However good the shows are, the ticket prices rarely match those for professional product. Some contemporary sources suggest that the productions at the *Tyne* actually lost money overall. One early supporter commented, 'I soon realised that the theatre is a black hole you throw money into, the more shows produced the greater the losses.' While the amateur productions may not have raised the money which some of those involved claim, what they most certainly did achieve was to return the *Tyne* to a place of live entertainment.

Investing in property

As well as mounting productions, the trust invested in property, raising finance initially against guarantees provided by supporters and later, on the security of the property it then owned. The returns on this investment helped subsidise the management costs. The trust bought the theatre in 1980 and then acquired the lease of the adjacent pub as well as the liquidated stock of a costumes hire company. Using this property as collateral, it proceeded to buy the whole block in which the theatre was sited. The block included five shops, two pubs, and a Chinese restaurant (with their related office accommodation) as well as six flats. The income from these properties was used to finance the loans and support the theatre operation. This property portfolio was seen as an 'endowment' fund which would guarantee the long-term future of the theatre.

How long the theatre could have continued as a predominantly 'amateur' operation, will never be known because, on Christmas Day 1985, fire broke out and the whole process was brought to a dramatic halt. The backstage, the stage itself and part of the proscenium arch were severely damaged, as was a large part of the roof. Under the stage, a meticulous salvage operation recovered most of the original fittings and some re-usable timber and Dr Wilmore returned once again to restore the machinery, rediscovering techniques of construction which had not been used for over one hundred years.

With the insurance money, the trust set about replacing the damaged structure and refurbishing the auditorium to a higher standard than it had previously been able to achieve. Eleven months later, the theatre reopened. The renovation work had been completed at a cost of £1.5 million.

By the time the *Tyne* reopened, its rival, the *Theatre Royal*, had closed for refurbishment so the *Tyne* was able to host many of its productions. Audiences were good and the income from the commercial investments was sufficient to provide the additional support needed. Once the *Royal* reopened, however, the scene changed. The deficit on the *Tyne*'s revenue budget began to increase and eat into the money needed to finance the debts which had been incurred to acquire the property portfolio.

The trust set about finding partners to share the cost of running the theatre.

Tyne and Wear Theatre moves in

During the 1980s, the concept of using the arts as regeneration agents in run-down city centre areas was gaining credence and cities such as Sheffield and Bradford had begun to develop successful 'arts quarters'. The Westgate area (which also housed the recently developed *Newcastle Arts Centre* complex and *Dance City*) began to be seen as such a quarter. The term 'Theatre Village' was coined with the *Tyne Theatre* identified as the core facility.

In 1987, Northern Arts, then headed by Peter Stark, directed over £750,000 (half the amount spent on Newcastle as

a whole) into projects in the Westgate area. Linked to this overall strategy, Northern Arts helped broker a deal whereby an existing repertory company, the Tyne and Wear Theatre Company then based at the 480-seat university owned *Playhouse Theatre*, was to move into the *Tyne Theatre*. The theatre company was already revenue funded. It was offered an increase of £60,000 a year (taking the annual grant to £444,000) as well as additional funding to facilitate the move. Towards the end of 1987, The Tyne and Wear Theatre Company signed a short-term lease on the building. A new artistic director was appointed – Andrew Mckinnon – drawn from his position as manager of the *Theatre Royal* in York. The intention was that he would, in time, head a company which would embrace both the Tyne and Wear Theatre Company and the New Tyne Theatre and Opera House Company (using the building for four to six weeks a year) as well as providing a regional base for the National Youth Theatre (four weeks a year).

But things did not work out as planned. The repertory company found itself unable to increase its audience numbers sufficiently to make the expected contribution towards the *Tyne*'s running costs. At the same time, its occupancy reduced the income which the theatre had previously earned from hiring out its premises. Conflicts of interest and clashes of personality between the amateurs and the professional arts administrators brought the agreement to an end before the operational difficulties could be resolved.

By 1989, the trust was back in the position of having a theatre to run without subsidy and without access to Arts Council supported touring product. Even with the income from its property investments, the operation was heading further into deficit. Bringing in the repertory company had exacerbated rather than improved the financial situation.

More property deals and another partnership

Once again the trust looked to its property interests to support the operation. It also continued the search for a partner organisation to contribute towards the theatre's running costs. These two objectives came together when an agreement was reached with the local College of Technology (now Newcastle College) to establish a performing arts training school within Waterloo house, an adjacent property owned by the theatre. The necessary alterations were completed by the summer of 1990 and the college's performing arts department took up occupation in the September of that year.

The relationship between the trust and the college proved

beneficial to both partners. The rent strengthened the trust's financial position while new facilities (which included use of the theatre) enabled the college to attract more students and extend the range and number of courses it offered.

The following year, an appeal was launched to raise money to extend Waterloo House to create additional teaching and rehearsal rooms. One of the patrons was Norma Major who had attended a Joan Sutherland Gala Charity Concert hosted by the theatre in aid of the Prince's Trust and had seen the work being done by the students. The appeal met its target and construction started in February 1992. Once again, the work was completed in time for the students to move in at the beginning of the September term.

Crash and aftermath

The trust then embarked on a further building project with a plan to develop the land to the west of the theatre to accommodate the expanding needs of the college. Part of the new building was to provide student bedrooms which would also be used to accommodate a summer school. Work started in 1993 and the shell of the building was soon completed. But this time the project hit cash flow problems. Hoped for grant assistance did not materialise and before the development reached the stage where it could start to generate the income to cover the capital investment costs, the trust was forced to put the whole operation into the hands of administrators. It owed Barclays Bank £1.3 million.

A rescue bid is launched

The first organisation to take an interest was the Tyne and Wear Building Preservation Trust with a proposal aimed at ensuring that the grade I listed building would be properly preserved and would continue to function as a live theatre. By this time, the National Lottery had been set up. The Building Preservation Trust put together a bid to secure funding from the Heritage Lottery Fund to buy the *Tyne Theatre* (and its income-providing performing arts facilities) from the administrators. The Architectural Heritage Fund declared its willingness to offer a short-term loan. Although the Heritage Lottery Fund had some doubts as to whether the Building Preservation Trust would be able to manage such a project and suggested that The Theatres Trust in London might be a more appropriate owner, it eventually agreed, in principle, to offer £475,000. The Arts Council of England earmarked £100,000 and intimated a willingness to

consider a further application for improvements to the front-of-house areas.

The lottery bid also served to give a new momentum to the concept of the 'Theatre Village' and an 'arts led' movement got underway to submit a much larger application based on the *Tyne Theatre* and much of the surrounding land. The proposal included a major new concert hall. Fears were expressed at the time that this initiative could adversely effect the *Tyne*, delaying the rescue bid by introducing a far more complicated set of considerations. With negotiations and consultations dragging on, The Theatres Trust urged the Heritage Lottery Fund to assess the Building Preservation Trust's application 'on its own merits'.

Enter Karl Watkin

While the heritage groups were looking at ways to acquire and preserve the building and the arts interests were developing their more ambitious plans, other people were beginning to put together packages which would enable them to acquire the *Tyne Theatre* and its portfolio of property.

Amongst these was Tyneside millionaire businessman, Karl Watkin, who planned to use the theatre as a national base for the D'Oyly Carte Opera Company and to create a 'centre of excellence' for lyric theatre. An article by Kevin Stephens in *Arts Management Weekly* (29 February 1996) outlines the scenario at the time.

> Watkin had raised promises of £250,000 subsidy a year guaranteed for five years from local sources. In addition there is an income stream of close to £200,000 per year generated by the theatre's established rental of its associated premises to Newcastle College. Watkin will himself underwrite a further income stream of £200,000 from the theatres associated businesses, mostly bars. The theory is that these sources of income will be sufficient to run the theatre and provide baseline subsidy level for the company.

Why should a businessman who, by his own admission, knew nothing about theatre and did not understand the arts, want to buy the *Tyne*? His explanation is that he was asked to do so (others say he volunteered) – as a holding operation to prevent it being acquired by other, less sympathetic, interests. Watkin's intention was that a new trust should be set up to manage (but not own) the property. Once this had been done, he planned to sell the theatre to the Tyne and Wear Building Preservation Trust. He anticipated owning the property for about two months. But it did not work out that way.

D'Oyly Carte, which has an operating base in Wolverhampton, blew hot and cold over the move to Newcastle. The company eventually decided against the move and the 'partnership' (Newcastle City Council, the Tyne Theatre, the Business Community and D'Oyly Carte) disintegrated with the key players each citing the unreasonable demands of the others as the reason for the collapse of the deal.

Whatever the rights and wrongs of the situation, Karl Watkin was left with a theatre and a contract requiring its continued operation. He had also acquired the shell of the performing arts building, the development which had led to the insolvency of the former owners. He set about completing this building so that it would generate the required income, carrying out repairs to the theatre which had been neglected during the crisis and getting the operation up and running.

With the building now in commercial ownership, the funds that would have been available for rescue – nearly £600,000 from the Arts Council and Heritage Lottery Funds and a loan of over £300,000 from the Architectural Heritage Fund, were lost. Although there were some discussions about transferring the theatre and its adjacent properties (the performing arts facilities) to a new charitable trust and allowing Karl Watkin to run it, nothing was resolved. Watkin was on his own.

A commercial operation?

Anne Palmer, a business partner of Karl Watkin, moved into the *Tyne Theatre* as its manager and bought in a consultant to advise on programming. Together they made 'all the mistakes which everybody makes'. Having found out how the accepted style of operation worked (or rather did not work when viewed in straight business terms), Anne Palmer began to apply her own ideas. She recognised that while the theatre had the acoustics of an opera house, the cultural base to support a second touring venue for 'art' product did not exist. She saw the business potential resting in the building being run as a community theatre and set out to draw in as wide a range of people as possible. What Anne Palmer found the Newcastle audiences wanted was 'bright lights, bright music, famous TV names, and a good feeling when you leave, with everybody clapping'.

Three main groups were targeted: families, children and, perhaps more surprisingly, disabled people. Contacts were established with groups working with disabled people and, when fully operational, the theatre was drawing in an audience of which ten to fifteen per cent were either mentally or physically disadvantaged. Families were encouraged by prices geared to providing an outing for a family of four for about £20. A children's club was set up with discounts, cards, and 'meet the cast' invitations and 'birthday' teas were arranged alongside children's productions. With the theatre's seven bars brought into operation and regular matinée performances, Anne Palmer claims to have got 6000 people through the doors in an average week, and, on occasions, to have been able to increase this figure to 15,000.

What she was not able to do was to make the operation pay. As many others had already discovered, buying in the product took virtually all the ticket income leaving nothing over for running costs, yet alone profit. The theatre business just would not work in business terms within the timescale which Karl Watkin had set himself. He decided to sell. When this publication went to press, discussions were taking place with a number of potential buyers including theatre managements, a businessman who intended to turn the building into a pub/music venue and the still to be formed 'trust' of arts interests (with the Performing Arts Centre having a key role).

During the time of his ownership, Watkin maintained the theatre building and honoured the previous owner's agreement with Newcastle College to improve the performing arts facilities in return for an increased rental. (The rental income during this period was used to offset the capital investment rather than subsidise the productions.) These improvements, alone, were estimated by Anne Palmer to have cost about £750,000. Watkin also tried to encourage the English Shakespeare Company's expressed interest in becoming the resident company at the *Tyne Theatre,* subsidising a working visit and production.

The Watkin operation was certainly not without its critics and there are those who would put a very different gloss on the events surrounding the purchase and subsequent management of the *Tyne* and its properties than that set out above.

What next?

The strategy which the Tyne Theatre and Opera Company developed, of building up a portfolio of income earning investments to provide revenue support for the theatre and of finding partners to share the cost of the operation and produce product, was conceptually a sound one. Given a slightly different set of circumstances, it might well have worked.

In 1995, when the administrators were considering the future of the building, John Earl, then Director of The Theatres Trust, wrote:

> With very few exceptions effective preservation depends on use. A theatre which has been converted for other purposes can become a sad memento of itself.

Unfortunately, the best 'self-preserving' use is often far from being commercially profitable. In these circumstances the historic building which has some form of endowment to make its future secure is uncommonly fortunate.

The greatest achievement of the (then) present custodians of the *Tyne Theatre* is that they have provided it with a property endowment.

The fear now is that the *Tyne* will be separated from its supporting properties. If this were to happen, it is difficult to see how the building could reopen as theatre. How much of the original property portfolio Karl Watkin actually bought, what remains in the package, and what is currently being offered for sale is not public knowledge. It is evident, however, that some of the portfolio was sold off during the trust's time in order to finance the developments. The corner pub, for instance, was no longer owned by the trust by the time the theatre and its properties were sold to Karl Watkin.

Those interested in the preservation of the theatre as a live performance venue hope that a new trust can be formed, that grants will be made available to enable it to buy and renovate the theatre, and that sufficient of the original property portfolio remains in the sales package to secure its future. Meanwhile, what will happen to the grade l listed building and its unique set of stage machinery remains an open question.

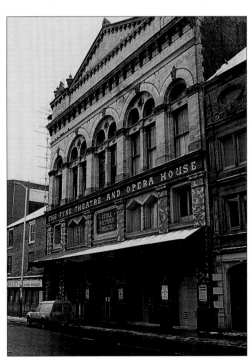

(Ian Grundy)

Key Points

- Grade I listed building with unique set of Victorian stage machinery
- Newcastle's second theatre
- Bought, refurbished and run by an amateur operatic society
- Supported by income from a property portfolio
- Partnerships established first with a subsidised repertory company and later with the performing arts unit of a nearby college
- Whole operation collapsed when a property development failed
- Rescue bids launched by heritage and arts interests
- Theatre and property portfolio bought by local entrepreneur
- Theatre reopened but is offered for sale three years later

Type of operation:
Receiving house with adjacent performing arts unit
(let to a college)
Ownership and management:
Owned and managed by Karl Watkin
Original architect:
1867 William Parnell
Listed:
Grade I
Uses:

1867–1919	*theatre*
1919–74	*cinema*
1974–79	*empty*
1979 continuing	*theatre*

Current capacity:
1100

1: Addresses and Contacts

Case Study Theatres

Alhambra Theatre
Morley Street
Bradford
West Yorkshire BD7 1AJ

Chipping Norton Theatre
2 Spring Street
Chipping Norton
Oxfordshire OX7 5NL

Edinburgh Festival Theatre
13/29 Nicholson Street
Edinburgh EH8 9FT

Georgian Theatre Royal
Victoria Road
Richmond
North Yorkshire DL10 4DW

Grand Theatre
Church Street
Blackpool FY1 1HT

Grand Theatre
St Leonardgate
Lancaster LA1 1NL

Hackney Empire
291 Mare Street
Hackney
London E8 1EJ

Lyceum Theatre
Norfolk Street
Sheffield
South Yorkshire S1 2LA

Mayflower Theatre
Commercial Road
Southampton SO15 1GE

Opera House
Quay Street
Manchester M3 3HP

Palace Theatre
Oxford Street
Manchester M1 6FT

Stephen Joseph Theatre
Westborough
Scarborough
North Yorkshire YO11 1JW

Theatre Royal
202 Hope Street
Glasgow G2 3QA

Tyne Theatre and Opera House
111 Westgate Road
Newcastle upon Tyne NE1 4AG

Theatre Advisory Bodies

*Association of British Theatre
Technicians (ABTT)*
47 Bermondsey Street
London SE1 3XT
Tel: 0171 403 3778

Cinema Theatre Association
56 Charrington Street
London NW1 1RD
Tel: 0171 387 0528

Save London's Theatres Campaign
Guild House
Upper St Martin's Lane
London WC2H 9EG

Society of Theatre Consultants
47 Bermondsey Street
London SE1 3XT
Tel: 0171 403 3778

The Theatres Trust
22 Charing Cross Road
London WC2H 0HR
Tel: 0171 836 8591

Arts Councils

(also responsible for the
distribution of National Lottery
funding for arts projects)

Arts Council of England
14 Great Peter Street
London SW1P 3NQ
Tel: 0171 333 0100

Arts Council of Northern Ireland
77 Malone Road
Belfast BT9 6AQ
Tel: 01232 385200

Arts Council of Wales
9 Museum Place
Cardiff CF1 3NX
Tel: 01222 376500

Scottish Arts Council
12 Manor Place
Edinburgh EH3 7DD
Tel: 0131 226 6051

Regional Arts Boards

Eastern Arts Board
Cherry Hinton Hall
Cherry Hinton Road
Cambridge CB1 4DW
Tel: 01223 215355

East Midlands Arts Board
Mountfields House
Forest Road
Loughborough LE11 3HU
Tel: 01509 218292

London Arts Board
Elme House
133 Long Acre
London WC2E 9AF
Tel: 0171 240 1313

Northern Arts Board
9–10 Osborne Terrace
Jesmond
Newcastle upon Tyne NE2 1NZ
Tel: 0191 281 6334

North West Arts Board
Manchester House
22 Bridge Street
Manchester M3 3AB
Tel: 0161 834 6644

Southern Arts Board
13 St Clement Street
Winchester SO23 9DQ
Tel: 01962 855099

South East Arts Board
Union House
Eridge Road
Tunbridge Wells
Kent TN4 8HF
Tel: 01892 507200

South West Arts Board
Bradninch Place
Gandy Street
Exeter EX4 3LS
Tel: 01392 218188

West Midlands Arts Board
82 Granville Street
Birmingham B1 2LH
Tel: 0121 631 3121

*Yorkshire and Humberside
Arts Board*
21 Bond Street
Dewsbury
West Yorks WF13 1AX
Tel: 01924 455555

Arts Organisations

*Association for Business
Sponsorship of the Arts (ABSA)*
Nutmeg House
60 Gainsford Street
Butlers Wharf
London SE1 2NY
Tel: 0171 378 8143

*Department for Culture,
Media & Sport*
2–4 Cockspur Street
London SW1Y 5DH
Tel: 0171 211 6000

English Regional Arts Boards
5 City Road
Winchester
Hampshire SO23 8SD
Tel: 01962 851063

Foundation for Sport & the Arts
PO Box 20
Liverpool L13 1HB
Tel: 0151 259 5505

Voluntary Arts Network
PO Box 200
Cardiff CF5 1YH
Tel: 01222 395395

Heritage Organisations

Architectural Heritage Fund
Clareville House
26/27 Oxenden Street
London SW1Y 4EL
Tel: 0171 925 0199

*CADW (Welsh Historic
Monuments)*
Brunel House
2 Fitzalan Road
Cardiff CF2 1UY
Tel: 01222 500200

The Civic Trust
17 Carlton House Terrace
London SW1Y 5AW
Tel: 0171 930 0914

Civic Trust for Wales
2nd Floor
Empire House
Mount Stuart Square
The Dodes
Cardiff CF1 6DN
Tel: 01222 484606

Department of the Environment
(Historic Monuments and
Buildings Branch)
5/33 Hill Street
Belfast BT1 2LA
Tel: 01232 235000

English Heritage
23 Saville Row
London W1X 1AB
Tel: 0171 973 3000

The Georgian Group
6 Fitzroy Square
London W1P 6DN
Tel: 0171 387 1720

Heritage Lottery Fund
7 Holbein Place
London SW1W 8NR
Tel: 0171 591 6000

Historic Scotland
Longmore House
Salisbury Place
Edinburgh EH9 1SH
Tel: 0131 668 8600

Save Britain's Heritage
70 Cowcross Street
London EC1M 6BP
Tel: 0171 253 3500

Scottish Civic Trust
The Tobacco Merchants House
42 Miller Street
Glasgow G1 1DT
Tel: 0141 221 1466

Twentieth Century Society
70 Cowcross Street
London EC1M 6BP
Tel: 0171 250 3857

*Ulster Architectural
Heritage Society*
66 Donegal Pass
Belfast BT7 1BU
Tel: 01232 550213

The Victorian Society
1 Priory Gardens
London W4 1TT
Tel: 0181 994 0815

Architecture and
Planning Institutions

*Royal Incorporation of Architects
in Scotland (RIAS)*
15 Rutland Square
Edinburgh EH1 2BE
Tel: 0131 229 7545/7205

Royal Institute of British Architects
(Clients Advisory Service)
66 Portland Place
London W1N 4AD
Tel: 0171 580 5533

*Royal Society of Architects
in Wales*
But Buildings
King Edward 7th Avenue
Cathays Park
Cardiff CF1 3NB
Tel: 01222 874753

Royal Society of Ulster Architects
2 Mount Charles
Belfast BT7 1NZ
Tel: 01232 323760

The Royal Town Planning Institute
26 Portland Place
London W1N 4BE
Tel: 0171 636 9107

Access

*The ADAPT Trust
(Access for Disabled People
to Arts Premises Today)*
8 Hampton Terrace
Edinburgh EH12 5JD
Tel: 0131 346 1999

ADAPT Northern Ireland
Disability Action
Albany House
2nd Floor
73–75 Great Victoria Street
Belfast BT2 7AF
Tel: 01232 231211

Disabilities Scotland
Princes House
5 Shandwick Place
Edinburgh EH2 4RG
Tel: 0131 229 8632

*Centre for Accessible
Environments (CAE)*
Nutmeg House
60 Gainsford Street
Butlers Wharf
London SE1 2NY
Tel: 0171 357 8182

Charity: Official Bodies

Charities Aid Foundation
Kings Hill
West Malling
Kent ME19 4TA
Tel: 01732 520000

*The Charity Commission for
England and Wales*
2nd Floor
20 Kings Parade
Queens Dock
Liverpool L3 4DQ
Tel: 0151 703 1515

Scottish Charities Office
The Crown Office
25 Chambers Street
Edinburgh EH1 1LA
Tel: 0131 226 2626

2: LEGISLATION

Consultative (theatres)

Theatres Trust Act 1976

Theatres Trust (Scotland) Act 1978

Town & Country Planning (General Development Procedure) Order 1995, Article 10, Para.5

The Town and Country Planning General Development (Scotland) Order 1992 (Article 15) as amended by *The Town & Country Planning (General Development Procedure) (Scotland) Amendment (No. 2) Order* 1994.

Disability access

(List of key documents compiled by Alan Richards, a retired Department of the Environment civil servant responsible for the 1995 Disability Act. Published in *The Theatres Trust Newsletter,* September 1997)

Building Regulations 1991: Section M and The Approved Document to Part M: revised October 1992

Access and facilities for disabled people. Approved Document M (HMSO)

Chronically Sick and Disabled Persons Act 1970

Chronically Sick and Disabled Persons (Amendment) Act 1976

The Disabled Persons Act 1981

The Town and Country Planning Act 1971

The Building Act 1984

BS 5810 (1979)

BS 5588: Part 8 (1988)

BS1 PD6523: 1989

Disability Discrimination Act 1995

The EU's Concept of Accessibility

Health and Safety

Fire Precautions Act 1971

Guide to Fire Precautions in Existing Places of Entertainment. Home Office (1990)

Building Act 1984

Building Regulations 1990

Building Standards (Scotland) Regulations 1990

Licensing Act 1964

Licensing (Scotland) Act 1976

Cinema Act 1985

Private Places of Entertainment Act 1968

Planning

Department of the Environment & Department of Culture, Media and Sport PPG15, *Planning Policy Guidance: Planning & the Historic Environment.* 1994. para 6.10. and 6.12.

Department of the Environment Circular 13/87, *Changes of Use of Buildings and Other Land: (the) Use Classes Order*, 1987

Historic Scotland (SDD): *Memorandum of Guidance on Historic Buildings and Conservation Areas,* 1988

Town & Country Planning (*Listed Buildings and Conservation Areas*) Act 1990

Town & Country Planning (*Use Classes*) *Order* 1987 (SI:1987 No. 764)

Town & Country Planning *General Development Procedure Order* 1995, Article 10, Para 5

Town & Country Planning *General Development (Scotland) Order* 1992

Procurement

The Public Services Contract Regulations 1993. (SI: 1993 No. 3228)

3: GUIDANCE NOTES

(available free of charge unless marked otherwise)

The Theatres Trust:

1. *Legal Basis and Planning Functions of the Trust*
2. *What is a Theatre?*
3. *Theatre Protection – How to Save a Theatre*
4. *Taking advice on Theatre Design and Preservation*

   (A full list of publications is available)

Arts Council of England

(A catalogue is available listing all the publications which the Arts Council distributes)

Arts Funding System Pack
Policy for Dance of the English Arts Funding System
Regional Dance Agencies
Theatre and Disability Conference Report
White Paper on Drama in England

English Heritage

Theatres: A guide to Theatre Conservation 1995

Scottish Civic Trust

How to start a Civic or Amenity Society

4: A SELECT BIBLIOGRAPHY

Compiled by Paul Iles

Most facets of theatre – architecture, scene design, literature and stage techniques – are well documented historically and in terms of current practice. British books dealing with theatre management are rare, and are soon out of print. Sources can be divided between those publications written for university study of arts administration; a mountainous 'arts funding body' list of policy reviews, investigations and reports; and memoirs or biographies of a few managers which record productions, casts and offer insight into management. They comprise a meagre library on theatre management.

The only comprehensive study of the organisation of touring theatres is Crispin Raymond, *Clear Sightlines*, Arts Council of Great Britain, London, 1993. This is indispensable and will be re-issued in an updated version in 1999: *Once More With Feeling!* He analyses aspects of success as financial, artistic, community, building and service, going on to suggest frameworks for monitoring success and debates public and private sector funding, organisational structures as well as offering financial and non-financial indicators. Raymond has also written on the touring theatre in *Beyond Survival,* 1991 and *The Balanced Theatre Revisited,* 1990 – both Arts Council publications. Raymond's *Members Matter,* Arts Council, 1992, is a useful manual about friends' and supporters' groups. For guidance on leadership at board level, see Timothy Pascoe and Paul Pia, *Care, Diligence and Skill: A Handbook for the Governing Bodies of Arts Organisations,* Scottish Arts Council, Edinburgh, 1995.

There are theatre management vade-mecums: Sheena Barbour (ed.), *British Performing Arts Yearbook,* Rhinegold, London, 1998 and

The Original British Theatre Directory, Richmond House Publishing, London, 1998. Periodicals include *The Arts Business, International Arts Manager* and *The Stage and Television Today.* The latter publishes an annual 'Venues' supplement.

Some academic journals are useful: *Arts Research Digest,* Research Services Unit, University of Newcastle upon Tyne or Oliver Bennett (ed.), *International Journal of Cultural Policy,* Warwick University. The Arts Councils and Regional Arts Boards issue publication lists of reports. These include *Review of Large Scale Touring: The Provision of Lyric Work in England,* Arts Council of England, London, 1998. Their *Arts Council News* gives monthly details of awards and schemes, including lists of Lottery capital grants. Other potential sources are annual reports and accounts, although few theatres publish these. Try Birmingham Hippodrome Theatre, Belfast Grand Opera House, Plymouth Theatre Royal, Mayflower Theatre Southampton or, for all theatres, Companies' House where some theatres lodge more than the statutory minimum requirements. Norwich Theatre Royal issues an annual economic impact study. There are several histories of individual theatres. These are listed by town in John Cavanagh, *British Theatre Bibliography, 1901–1985,* Motley Press, Mottisfont, 1989. Management organisations issue newsletters to member theatres and companies: try The Theatrical Management Association, Society of London Theatre and The Independent Theatre Council.

Only a small selection of a larger field for theatre planning and architecture is given. It includes work on cinema buildings since many of these are used for live theatre. The Association of British Theatre Technicians issues a relevant newsletter. Back issues of their defunct journal *Sightline* contain valuable technical reviews of theatres. See also *The Theatres Trust Newsletter* (quarterly) and annual reports for opinion, features and nationwide news of theatre buildings. The Theatres Trust also issues *Advice Notes* on topics such as how to set about protecting a threatened theatre and (with English Heritage) *A Guide to Theatre Preservation.* The Arts Council Lottery Division has published a range of guidance notes, publications and videos. The Voluntary Arts Network helps theatres making Lottery applications through publications such as *Business Planning, Community Benefit* and *Converting Buildings for Arts Use.*

The following additional titles are helpful to people considering the building and operation aspects of new and restored theatres. North American titles cited are those readily available in the United Kingdom.

Theatre Management and Economics

William J. Byrnes, *Management and the Arts,* Focal Press, Boston and London, 1993.

Anne-Marie Doulton, *The Arts Funding Guide,* Directory of Social Change, London, 1991.

Marian Fitzgibbon and Anne Kelly (eds), *From Maestro to Manager: Critical Issues in Arts and Culture Management,* Oak Tree Press, Dublin, 1997.

Vivian Freakley and Rachel Sutton, *Essential Guide to Business in the Performing Arts,* Hodder & Stoughton, London, 1996.

Michael Hammett, *Touring Theatre in the Age of Mass Media,* John Offord, Eastbourne, 1980.

Philip Kotler and Joanne Scheff, *Standing Room Only: Strategies for Marketing the Performing Arts,* Harvard Business School Press, Boston, 1997.

John Myerscough, *The Economic Importance of the Arts in Britain,* Policy Studies Institute, London, 1988.

John Pick, *The Theatre Industry: Subsidy, Profit and the Search for New Audiences,* Comedia, London, 1985.

John Pick and M. Anderton, *Arts Administration,* E & F N Spon, London, 1985.

Francis Reid, *Theatre Administration,* Adam & Charles Black, London, 1983.

Alvin H. Reiss, *Don't Just Applaud – Send Money! The Most Successful Strategies for Funding and Marketing the Arts,* Theatre Communications Group, New York, 1995.

Brian Rix (Lord Rix of Whitehall), *Tour de Farce: A Tale of Touring Theatres and Strolling Players,* Hodder & Stoughton, London, 1992.

Richard E. Schneider and Mary Jo Ford, *The Well Run Theatre: Systems for Daily Operation,* Drama Book Publishers, New York, 1993.

Elizabeth Sweeting, *Theatre Administration,* Pitman, London, 1969.

John Vasey, *Tour Production Management: How to Take Your Show on the Road*, Focal Press, Newton and London, 1998.

Harold L. Vogel, *Entertainment Industry Economics: A Guide for Financial Analysis*, Cambridge University Press, Cambridge, 1998.

Theatre Planning, Architecture and Access

Ian Appleton, *Access to Arts Buildings: Provision for People with Disabilities – Management Policy and Design Standards,* Scottish Arts Council, Edinburgh, 1996.

Stanley Bell, Norman Marshall and Richard Southern, *Essentials of Stage Planning,* Frederick Muller, London, 1949.

Christopher Brereton, David F. Cheshire, John Earl, Victor Glasstone, Iain Mackintosh, Michael Sell, *Curtains!!! or A New Life for Old Theatres,* John Offord, Eastbourne, 1982.

Marvin Carlson, *Places of Performance: The Semiotics of Theatre Architecture,* Cornell University Press, Ithaca and London, 1989.

Nicholas Crickhowell, *Opera House Lottery: Zaha Hadid and the Cardiff Bay Project,* University of Wales Press, Cardiff, 1997.

Mark Foley, *Dance Spaces,* Arts Council of Great Britain, London, 1994.

Michael Forsyth, *Auditoria: Designing for the Performing Arts,* Mitchell Publishing, London, 1987.

Victor Glasstone, *Victorian and Edwardian Theatres: An Architectural and Social Survey,* Thames and Hudson, London, 1975.

Richard Gray, *One Hundred Years of Cinema Architecture,* Lund Humphries and the Cinema Theatre Association, London, 1997.

Roderick Ham, *Theatres: Planning Guidance for Design and Adaptation,* Butterworth Architecture, London, 1988.

Stephen Joseph, (ed.), *Actor and Architect,* University of Manchester, Manchester, 1964.

Andreas Kaldor, *Opera Houses of Europe,* Antique Collectors' Club, London, 1996.

Richard and Helen Leacroft, *Theatre and Playhouse: An Illustrated Survey of Theatre Building from Ancient Greece to the Present Day,* Methuen, London, 1984.

Richard Leacroft, *The Development of the English Playhouse: An Illustrated Survey of Theatre Building in England from Medieval to Modern Times,* Methuen, London, 1988.

Richard Leacroft, *Civic Theatre Design,* Dennis Dobson, London, 1949.

Iain Mackintosh, *Architecture, Actor and Audience,* Routledge, London, 1993.

Ronnie Mulryne and Margaret Shewring, *Making Space for Theatre: British Architecture and Theatre Since 1945,* Mulryne and Shewring Ltd, Stratford upon Avon, 1995.

David Naylor and Joan Dillon, *American Theatres: Performance Halls of the Nineteenth Century,* John Wiley, New York, 1997.

Edwin O. Sachs and Ernest Woodrow, *Modern Opera Houses and Theatres,* London, 1896–98, Arno Press, New York, 1981.

Richard Southern, *Proscenium and Sightlines: A Complete System of Stage Planning,* Faber and Faber, London, 1949.

James Steele, *Theatre Builders,* Academy Editions, London, 1996.

Judith Strong, *Building for the Arts,* Arts Council of Great Britain, London, 1990.

Judith Strong, *Winning by Design: Architectural Competitions,* Butterworth Heinemann, London, 1996.

Brian Walker, (ed.), *Frank Matcham, Theatre Architect,* Blackstaff Press, Belfast, 1980.